"A Doctor in Little Lhasa: One Year in Dharamsala with the Tibetans in Exile"

by

Timothy H. Holtz, M.D.

First published by Dog Ear Publishing
4010 W. 86th Street, Ste H
Indianapolis, IN 46268
www.dogearpublishing.net

ISBN: 978-159858-883-5

This book is printed on acid-free paper.

Printed in the United States of America

Cover Photo: Young Tibetan monk in the main Tsuglagkhang Temple, Lhasa, Tibet.

Dedicated to all my patients at Delek Hospital,
who taught me wisdom, patience, and compassion

Acknowledgments

I would be remiss if I did not first thank Sherry Rauh, my initial editor, without whom the first draft of this manuscript would never have seen the light of day. She urged me to put emotions to words, and to think about the structure of how to tell this year-long story. Several friends provided very helpful comments, among them Vern Faillettaz, Paran Pordell, Heather Joseph, Brandon Kohrt, Ameena Ahmed, Tetyana Keeble, Greta Anderson, and Nandini Selvam. I would like to thank them for taking time out of their busy schedules to provide comments on earlier drafts of this manuscript, as they assisted in improving the text. My loving sisters, Teri Holtz Young and Tracy Rock, also provided comments on conceptual "drafty" versions. Teri Sivilli, Abigail Wright, and Larry and Nonnie Crook provided thoughtful insights on Western interaction with Tibetans in exile, and sent helpful feedback to me during this process. Without Ann Lanner and Regina Bess all the words and graphics would not have come together. Elizabeth Fabel deserves heartfelt recognition. Special thanks go to Tsetan Dorje Sadutshang for his endless support throughout my year as a staff physician at Delek Hospital, and for his continued friendship and mentorship. I will be forever indebted to all the nurses at Delek Hospital for their never-ending patience and dedication to improving the health of Tibetans living in exile. Lastly, special thanks go to His Holiness the Dalai Lama, for making it all possible.

Preface

As the Chinese proverb attributed to Lao-tzu goes, "A journey of a thousand miles begins with a single step." The modern corollary, however, is often left out: "Make sure you don't stumble on the first step." It was the feeling that soon I would be a "real doctor," as my friends told me what happens when medical training is over, that made me cognizant of my immediate future. And a bit anxious to be sure not to stumble. I was finishing my senior year of residency in primary care internal medicine, and my 3-year on-the-job training was nearly over. I was supposedly ready to brave the new world of American medicine with the best training one could have, with a residency spent at one of the premier training grounds in the world for new physicians, in the heart of the medical mecca of Boston/Cambridge. During my training, however, I became progressively more interested in the health problems of immigrants and refugees in Cambridge, where I had my primary care practice clinic. Cambridge is home to persons of many nationalities, but especially Haitians, Ethiopians, Somalis, Portuguese, Brazilians, and Cape Verdeans. The health problems that occur in their communities are not treated much differently than they are in the general population, but immigrants and refugees do have health issues that often arise that require knowledge and sensitivity to each group's unique culture. It was a lesson I had learned as an intern, 2 years previously, when an elderly Haitian man had suffered a heart attack after months of chest pain that went untreated in our clinic. His cardiac symptoms were dismissed because, amidst a group of other somatic complaints, he used to say quite simply that he was "heartsick." He was diagnosed as yet another refugee in our clinic with depression. His case stuck with me, because I knew we could have served him better. I soon realized that what I really wanted to do was to get to know one population well, to serve them as a physician but also to be a student of their culture. I wanted to move abroad and become immersed.

I first became interested in international health during my first year of medical school. Having entered with a well rounded liberal arts college education, I soon realized how narrow my medical training was going to be. While understanding calcium metabolism and the function of the distal kidney tubule are conceptually important, so is the recognition of the social, environmental, and political factors that affect the health of communities. My perspective pulled me toward my professors in the preventive medicine department, who encouraged me to take a year off and attend public health school after my second year of medical studies. Studying for a master's degree in international health built the foundation of skills that I was seeking, and opened up new avenues of understanding health and illness in the world. I returned to finish medical school, but did so with fourth-year electives in community health care in international settings. I was able to study primary health care in Kathmandu, as well as community health and drug abuse in urban Karachi, Pakistan. During residency, I had also spent a short medical elective working in Khayelitsha, the vast informal housing "township" settlement outside Cape Town. These stints, however, were only for 2 months each, and seemed more like "medical tourism" to me. Halfway through training I realized that by the time I would finish my residency program, I would be ready to move abroad. I felt a need to get closer to community work.

During my second year of residency I applied for a fellowship in health and human rights from the Center for the Study of Society and Medicine at the Columbia University College of Physicians and Surgeons. The center had been sponsoring medical students to spend short electives abroad studying refugee and community health, but they had recently received funding to sponsor post-graduate physicians to live and work for a full year in a refugee community that had suffered from human rights abuses. When I applied I had specifically mentioned I was interested in going back to work in Asia. Therefore, I was naturally pleased when I was offered a post to live and work in a Tibetan refugee community in India in both a medical and public health capacity. A full year would fulfill my personal interest in understanding not only the infectious causes of ill health, but help a community that had suffered from decades of human rights abuses.

Following the end of my residency, 1994–1995, I lived and worked for a full year in Dharamsala, "The Peaceful Resting Place," in the northern Himalayan Indian state of Himachal Pradesh. This book is my story of that year. Dharamsala is in truth a peaceful but bustling little town, mainly due to its identity as the home of the Tibetan Government-in-Exile. In 1959 the Dalai Lama fled Tibet after being given advance warning of an impending kidnapping attempt of himself and his cabinet. After several weeks of crossing the Himalayas in disguise with a small party of devoted followers, he was able to reach safety in India and was given political exile from the invading Chinese army. In 1962 the Dalai Lama was offered a home in exile in Dharamsala, Himachal Pradesh, but it has been a restless stay owing to the drastic changes in his home country. What followed was more than 40 years of occupation by China of the sovereign country of Tibet, and the resultant deaths of millions of Tibetans from forced relocation, starvation, and repression. Over 100,000 Tibetans have followed the Dalai Lama into exile, with most of them now living in southern and northern India.

Delek Hospital ("delek" means "good health" in Tibetan) was dedicated by the Tibetan Government-in-Exile in 1971 to serve the growing medical needs of Tibetan refugees living in India. It was formed under the direction of Tsewang Rinchen Rishing, who saw the need for an allopathic Tibetan-run health care facility. The Dalai Lama gave his blessing for the initial construction, which consisted of a modest two-room clinic on a small plot of land on the Dharamsala hillside. It predominantly provides care to those refugees who are allowed to settle in the remote northern Indian state of Himachal Pradesh, estimated to be between 10,000–15,000.[1]

---

[1] There is another Tibetan Hospital in Mundgod settlement in the southern state of Karnataka. It serves the health needs of the first wave of nearly 80,000 Tibetans who fled Tibet and were relocated there during the early 1960s, as well as the needs of continuously newly arriving refugees who are resettled there (via Nepal and India).

The hospital, or "Delek" as it is known to the locals, is located adjacent to the Tibetan Government-in-Exile's compound (Gangchen Kyishong), and has a beautiful view of the Himachal Valley below. Initially, Delek Hospital was staffed by only 5 people, including one part-time Indian physician. Over time the demand for services grew, and the inpatient and outpatient structures were renovated to expand the available space. Basic laboratory and radiology suites were added in 1979 and 1981, respectively. During my year of service it was a 40-bed hospital with three wards, and was efficiently run by a small team of extremely dedicated Tibetans. There were roughly 15 full-time employees who staffed the various departments, namely administration, inpatient services, outpatient clinic, public health, tuberculosis control program and clinic, eye care, dental care, pharmacy, and laboratory and radiology services. Six nurses and four nursing assistants made up the core of the care delivered there, and they were assisted by a laboratory technician and two pharmacists. Unfortunately, the hospital was only able to attract, at most, one Tibetan allopathic physician[2] to work there at any one time. A modest procedure room was equipped to handle small-scale procedures, such as minor lacerations, chest tube placements, and casting of uncomplicated fractures. Routine deliveries could also be performed. There were about 15 inpatient beds in the general ward and 20 in the tuberculosis ward. The outpatient clinic saw about 40–60 patients per day. The hospital was full most of the time with sick Tibetans, local Indian patients, and the occasional tourist who was nonimmune to many of the diseases that the Indian subcontinent dishes out.

For those readers who are not familiar with the region, Tibet is a mountainous country in the northern Himalayas between India and China. It has been home to the nomadic Tibetan people for more than

---

[2] Allopathic medicine is defined as the dominant model of medical care delivered in Western industrialized society, based on a biomedical model of illness that relies on the treatment of disease through the use of natural and synthesized pharmaceuticals. This is in contrast to what is often called "traditional medicine," which often uses herbal and natural medicine, although by no means is that term used to connote "old fashioned."

one thousand years. After emerging in the mid-seventh century as a dynamic power holding sway over inner Asia, they fell under the subjugation of the Mongol rulers of the Yuan Dynasty in the 13th and 14th centuries, and later under the Manchu rulers of China's Qing Dynasty from the 18th to the 20th century. However, neither dynasty politically attached Tibet to China. The language, culture, and social mores of Tibet are distinctly different from those of China. Tibetan language has its roots in Sanskrit, from its southern neighbor India. In fact, during the hundreds of years between the Mongols and the Manchus, the Ming Dynasty (1368–1644) had very little contact with Tibet. Likewise, when the Qing Dynasty collapsed in 1911, Tibet became a closed society, and had very little contact with either the West or the East. Between the 17th century and 1959, the year when the current Dalai Lama (Tenzin Gyatso) fled Tibet, there is credible historical documentation that the Dalai Lama was the head of the Tibetan government. His Holiness the Dalai Lama now presides as the head of the Central Tibetan Administration of the Tibetan Government-in-Exile, located in Dharamsala, India. The Tibetan Government-in-Exile is not recognized by the United Nations as a displaced state, although it does act as the de facto administration for all exiled Tibetans.

I had set several goals for myself for the year I spent at Delek Hospital. First, I wanted to hone my medical skills, especially my diagnostic acumen, instead of relying on high-tech tests. In our age of expensive and often unnecessary medical procedures, many physicians no longer take the time to properly examine a patient and listen to his or her symptoms. Yet patients can tell doctors so much about what is wrong with them physically. I have heard anecdotally that well over half of medical conditions can be correctly diagnosed by an astute diagnostician who listens to the human body, smells the odor of illness, or notices the telltale signs of a specific disease. Ultimately, a year without CT scans and expensive blood tests would properly test my medical training.

Second, I wanted to serve a marginalized and neglected population. I deeply wanted to find a way to help the Tibetan community at large. I wanted to have a more lasting impact than handing out temporary treatments to ill persons in the clinic. My ultimate goal was to leave something behind that would continue to benefit the entire community.

Third, and related to the second, I wanted to learn more about community health in the field, and put my nascent knowledge of public health to use. The Tibetan refugee community in northern India is dispersed throughout the state of Himachal Pradesh, which calls for a public health system that is not overly reliant on direct provision of medical care. This would be the most challenging goal, because public health is frequently understaffed and underresourced. This is even more true in a refugee setting, as well as for the Tibetan refugee diaspora.

Lastly, I wanted to contribute to the new emerging field of "health and human rights." Broadly defined, the concept of health and human rights states that for people to be healthy, their core human rights need to be respected and fulfilled. Just as health is determined by so much more than medical care, there is an emerging consensus by many public health experts that there is an intrinsic connection between respect for people's fundamental rights and their ability to enjoy the highest possible standard of health. This connection was first identified in the late 1980s, when public health activists lobbied for the protection of the human rights of people living with HIV/AIDS as a necessary element of the international response to the growing pandemic.[3]

After HIV/AIDS, the lens was turned on many other health conditions with a fundamental link to human rights. My specific interest was in helping the Tibetan survivors of torture who were lucky enough to make it out of Tibet alive. They needed both medical and psychiatric assessment and treatment, but also recognition of the rights that had been violated. Living in exile after having been tortured in one's country is a difficult life, and can easily break one's

---

[3] For one of the first academic references to health and human rights, see Mann JM, Gostin L, Gruskin S, Brennan T, Lazzarini Z, Fineberg H. (1994). Health and human rights. *Health and Human Rights*, 1, 6-23.

spirit. The "health and human rights" component of their stories needed to be told.

The motivations to tell my story are simple. Firstly, I want to urge all young health professionals who might happen to read this to follow their heart, and serve a neglected community with their skills. One need not know how to put in a chest tube, treat TB, or deliver a child to make an impact in a small community whose health rights are not being recognized or fulfilled. There are many community health priorities that go unanswered in nearly every corner of the globe. Take the year off that you have always wanted to, and "follow your bliss." The time is now.

For those reading this who have a dedicated interest in the plight of Tibetan refugees and were curious about what it was like living among them, I hope these stories shed light on a fascinating and inspiring community. I would urge you to donate time and/or money in any way possible to assist their cause. Tibetan refugees are just like any other refugee population, with both physical and mental health needs. They need our assistance. The end of the book includes ways you can help.

All the stories in this memoir are of real people. In the majority of cases, the names have been changed to protect their right to confidentiality. Some people specifically asked me to use their real names, in order for their stories to be heard. My lasting hope in writing this book is that they are.

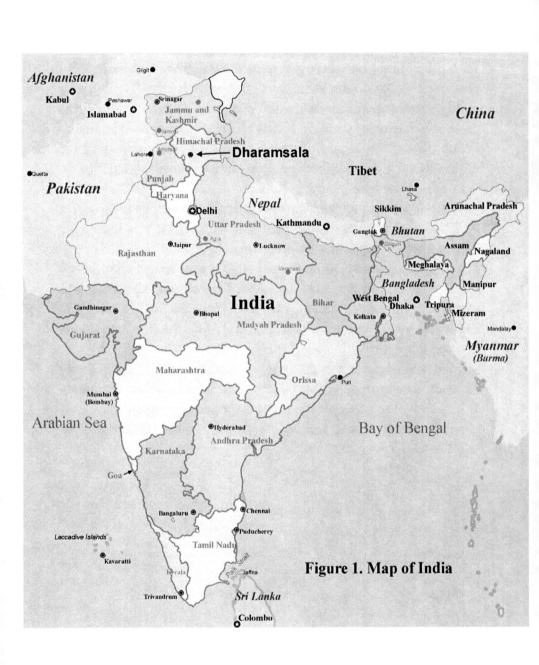

Figure 1. Map of India

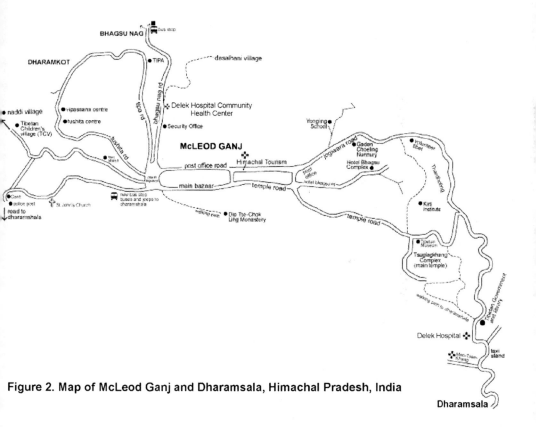

Figure 2. Map of McLeod Ganj and Dharamsala, Himachal Pradesh, India

Arrival

I had long wanted to be on this plane, a plane taking me back to India, a country I had fallen in love with as a senior college student studying abroad. I had made a vow back then to myself and to the country that had taught me about love and beauty, poverty and squalor, and the wealth of the spirit within, that I would return to repay the favor and give something back. As we neared landing, the bird's-eye view of the million morning fires of Delhi sent my heart back 8 years, to the moment when I first set foot in India. I remembered a squalid morass, the acrid smell of heavy air full of rancid odors, the sight of everything painted with the brilliant colors of red and yellow, the startling sight of crowds of humanity merging into one, and poverty unlike anything I had seen before. People everywhere. The image of entire families living, cooking, eating, and sleeping in the streets or in dismal squatter camps had never left me. Now, as the plane made its descent into Delhi International Airport, I saw those same families huddled around their morning fires, warming their hands and preparing their daily batch of chai tea. It occurred to me that their situation probably had not changed much over the years, although mine had.

During my first encounter with India, I was a wide-eyed student on an academic journey of discovery, studying religion and politics and traveling the subcontinent from the Himalayan foothills to Cape Comorin, ready to be cheated and amazed at every turn. I was 21 years old, about to graduate, and ready to experience the world. I had soaked in all the sights and sounds and people, and ultimately realized how much I was receiving. It was so much more than I could ever give back. This time I came as a medical volunteer backed up with a general medicine residency training and the desire to make a difference. I wanted to serve in a place that would require my full attention, and not be distracted by bombardment from outside distractions and influences. I wanted to focus, and focus diligently on healing the sick. I was eager to put my new skills to use in the country that had moved and inspired me years earlier.

Deciding to leave my country for a year was not as easy as I might make it out to be. For one thing, it meant not seeing my immediate family for many months, if not for the entire year. The last time I had spent any length of time in a foreign country, Haiti, there had been a coup; the entire country, including communications, had shut down. My mother didn't hear from me for several weeks — we were holding out in the countryside without safe passage back to the capital, and she thought I had perished with the other demonstrators. At one point after my return, she admitted that she envisioned my career would take me into the interior of Africa, never to be seen again. I assured her that several decades back, communication tools like e-mail did not exist, but now the entire world was getting wired in and we would likely be able to talk at least once per week. Leaving the airport terminal and getting on the plane was the hardest part; once you are airborne, the thrill of the adventure takes over. As we were taking off I threw a ceremonial goodbye kiss to my home and gazed at the clouds.

In some ways, I was not alone. I had several friends who had been accepted into the same health and human rights fellowship and were uprooting themselves as well to go live in other exotic locales. One close colleague had secured a fellowship with a nongovernmental organization, Physicians for Human Rights, to do health and human rights work in Cambodian prisons. Another was going to spend a year investigating the psychiatric needs of the poor in Egypt. My closest friend, also in the health and human rights fellowship, was working on lining up a position on the Thai-Burmese border, delivering medical care to a refugee population that had been fighting for human rights for decades against the Burmese military junta. We all promised to keep in touch. It was about to become a unique year of discovery and service for each of us in our own way. As the plane touched down in India, I felt a jolt of satisfaction. I had kept my promise to return.

Two days and worlds away from my home, the permeating odor of Delhi assaulted me outside the airport – an amalgam of sweat, grass, dirt, excrement, garbage, and the sweet smell of the tropics, all rolled into one. I took refuge in the taxi that would take me north to my new home. For the next year I would be safe in a small Tibetan refugee community in the foothills of the Himalayas. But first, I had to survive the drive from Delhi.

The trip took more than 10 hours on two-lane roads. Every few minutes, a truck sped towards my taxi in the wrong lane, its horn blaring, tassels waving, blue- and red-faced gods or gurus staring down from their portraits above the cab. One came so razor-close the TATA logo on its grill seemed the size of my fist. My driver finished overtaking his smaller vehicle prey and swerved out of our lane at the last possible second. I saw 10 accidents during the first 5 hours. Overturned trucks were everywhere, their contents scattered across the road and the fields beyond. There were propane canisters lying in heaps by the road, and metal poles sticking out of the ground. I saw large piles of rice and wheat and barley, metal industrial doodads of all shapes and sizes, and boxes of clothing in various states of destruction. It looked like a bazaar rather than a highway.

As we entered the northern Indian state of Himachal Pradesh, the flat, verdant terrain slowly gave way to rolling hills and river valleys with narrow bridges crossing over gurgling brooks. The scene was idyllic. We had entered the foothills of the Himalayas. Farming was still the staple work here, and the fields were full of women ankle deep in water planting rice. Children played with thin hoops of steel, hitting them with sticks to make them go up and down the steep paths visible from the road. I suddenly felt more free, like I wanted to get out of the taxi and walk through the villages that we drove past so quickly.

Four more hours and we arrived in Dharamsala,[4] called "Little Lhasa" by some observers, after the capital of Tibet. The road leading to Dharamsala snaked up the side of a mountain. We passed a few

---

[4] In Hindi the proper spelling and pronunciation of the town is "Dharam*shala*" with an "h," but in English and the Tibetan community the "h" is commonly dropped.

large hotels, a military base, and a typical village bazaar. The Indian part of town did not seem to stand out; it looked like any other Indian town. There were no visible signs of a Tibetan refugee presence at all – no prayer flags, no Buddhist stupas, and no Tibetan people. Finally we came to a fork in the road, and began to climb higher. After a while the town below became only a spot on the hillside. At 4,700 feet, the scene changed drastically, with pine trees replacing the deciduous trees. We suddenly came to Gangchen Kyishong, "The Happy Valley of Snow," center of the Tibetan Government-in-Exile. A large yellow and white portal, a gate into this new world, stood at the entrance. Through the gate I saw the cluster of buildings that made up the refugee Government-in-Exile, behind the main structure of learning they call the Tibetan Library. It was a small, unassuming, but grand little town.

The exiled government and several monasteries were rebuilt here after the Dalai Lama's flight to India in 1959, and the region had become a refuge for Tibetans fleeing Chinese rule. The Dalai Lama was welcomed to India with mostly positive feelings, although the Indian government was initially wary about offending its neighbor to the north by granting safe haven to the then unknown spiritual leader of 6 million people. Since that time, the Dalai Lama has become an international spiritual leader, not only in the contemporary movement for nonviolent resistance, but also in his life's work for a more peaceful and ordered global community. In 1989 the Dalai Lama was awarded the Nobel Peace Prize for his development of a philosophy of peace, and advocacy for nonviolent social change "based on tolerance and mutual respect in order to preserve the historical and cultural heritage of his people." The plight of the Tibetan people and their fight for self-determination has attracted many followers in the West, among me. For the most part, their refugee stay in India had been positive, although there had been some ripples along the way. Personally, I was glad to finally reach the home of the inspiring man they call the "Ocean of Wisdom" and his fellow Tibetans in need of a community health doctor.

After the taxi climbed further I got a glimpse of my new home, Tibetan Delek Hospital. The road curved up and around the bright blue building, leading to a main entrance on the hospital's third floor. The structure seemed to be attached to and detached from the hillside at the same time. One quick shake of the earth from a Himalayan quake seemed to be all that was needed to send the building sliding down the hill. True to the generosity of Tibetans, I received a brief but warm welcome from the hospital director, Dr. Tsetan Dorje Sadutshang. Dr. Tsetan, as he preferred to be called, had been the director for over 5 years, and had built a reputation for being a very skilled clinician and an able administrator. He had received public health training from Harvard University and frequent invitations to lecture in the U.S. From our brief initial chat, it was clear he understood both the clinical aspects of health in the tropics, as well as the public health interventions necessary to prevent disease and promote health in a refugee community.

I toured the small but comprehensive facilities, impressive in their scope given that we were in a rural environment, far from any high-tech referral medical centers. The first floor housed an outpatient clinic, dentistry and denture rooms, and some staff quarters. The entire second floor was devoted to the tuberculosis (TB) ward, where some patients had to stay for months. Many had decorated the dull white walls by taping pictures and photographs above their metal cots. The third floor handled just about everything else, from labor and delivery to typhoid and pneumonia, while the fourth floor housed the hospital offices and quarters for more staff and volunteers. The apartments for the volunteer doctors were situated along the top balcony, with an interior door into the front room and a window at the back. Apartment #1 had just been vacated by a departing Tibetan allopathic physician, so I was shown to the corner "studio" that would be my home for the next year. I simultaneously felt anxious and excited. Did I realize what I was getting myself into? Spending one year in a remote hospital in India, far from any tertiary care, would be an enormous challenge.

My bedroom and living space was not much bigger than a standard walk-in closet. The bed took up half the space. To make up for the room's small size, I had a spectacular view out my side window. The rear window overlooked the road behind the hospital, but the other faced west over the airy Gangetic Plains and lush hills set against the backdrop of the white-capped Dhauladhar Range. As I took my first look outside, monsoon clouds were gathering in the distance. Several hawks and kites soared over the hilltops, and a flock of parakeets traced a green wave across the sky. At the base of the hospital, a group of monkeys foraged for scraps. The realization that I had arrived finally set in. Though it was a small space, I was happy to have my own little refuge. What a thrill to be back in India!

The following morning of my first day, the hospital staff and volunteers packed the conference hall for a special event. Though tired, I found my curiosity was stronger than my jet lag. I took a seat between a couple of British volunteers and a Canadian Buddhist monk. A treasured lama from Kham, the northeastern province of Tibet, was about to give a *puja,* or ritual teaching and cleansing.

"He's doing the 'Medicine Buddha' *puja*," one of the other volunteers explained. "It's never been done at Delek Hospital."

I watched the TB patients with their masks on gather outside to listen through the open window. They seemed to scarcely notice the rain.

The lama began the ritual – in Tibetan, of course.

"He is invoking various spirits," whispered Alex the Canadian Buddhist monk. "Now he is asking us to visualize the Medicine Buddha floating over our heads."

I was thankful to have a translator. Over the next hour and a half, I learned that the Medicine Buddha teaches us to value compassion and knowledge, but to know our own limits. We can't solve all medical problems.

"Sometimes," the lama said, "you must allow the patient to let go of the Earth and join the cycle of death and rebirth." He then encouraged the Tibetans to recite the Medicine Buddha mantra 15 times a day:

Om Diata Be Kan Zey Be Kan Zey
Maha Be Kan Zey Be Kan Zey
Ranza Samu Gatey Swaha

I was grateful I to have arrived in time to receive the lama's teaching. The ceremony started a year that would change me, challenge me, and ultimately enlighten me both personally and professionally in this remote refugee setting. What seemed particularly relevant to our small hospital with limited resources (or to any health facility provider for that matter) was the message that there are some things doctors cannot fix, and some they can, and that the wisdom lies in knowing the difference. Above all, death should not be feared.

During my first night on call the next day, however, fear was exactly what I felt. My stomach was queasy and my legs a bit shaky, just as I had felt during my first call night as a medical intern, 3 years before. This time around, I had limited backup. Nothing in Cambridge had prepared me for the challenges of practicing medicine in a developing-country hospital, where I no longer had experienced attending physicians to turn to during a crisis. It wasn't a war zone, with bombs going off in the distance, that raised my anxiety. Quite the opposite, it was very still and quiet. Yet the burden was heavy, knowing that responsibility for each patient ultimately lay with me, that my decisions would be the ones of consequence.

Tibetans do not arrive in India with health insurance. For the roughly 3,000-4,000 who make the difficult journey over the Himalayan mountain passes into Nepal every year, health problems are common. Some are treated in Kathmandu, but the majority go straight to India in order to pass through Dharamsala and take a chance at seeing the Dalai Lama. Tibetans sorely lack health equity. Not only is health care difficult to access, but the availability and affordability of health care is lacking for them in India. And they suffer from this. That's where Delek Hospital steps in.

The hospital was well equipped, which put me somewhat at ease among familiar surroundings. Our triage room had a desk, a bench for waiting patients, and a cabinet full of emergency medical supplies. Behind it there was a small room with an examining table and clean white sheets, a shelf with the equipment needed to examine all the major body systems, and a clean sink with soap (a luxury in some villages). Down the corridor we had a room with a cot and chairs that was used for short overnight patient stays, rehydrating an ill person, or examining a patient too ill to make it to the doctor's office. Beyond that lay the procedure room, complete with operating table, X-ray viewing boxes, sinks, bottles of oxygen, and an emergency "crash cart" with supplies in case someone went into shock or collapsed.

The laboratory was downstairs, and was better equipped than I expected. The technician, Sonam, was well versed in the art of special microbiology color staining of feces for intestinal parasites and other microbes, could perform basic blood electrolyte tests, and even was the technician for the X-ray machine.

My first case on call was a monk with signs of severe calcium deficiency. He had been complaining of muscle cramps for weeks, and some mild shortness of breath, but what finally made him come to see us were the muscle spasms in his legs and some tingling at the tips of his fingers and toes. We had to treat the problem without being sure of just how low his calcium levels were. His potassium was reported by our laboratory as extremely low, basically incompatible with human life. I immediately felt that I might not be able to have 100% faith in the few pieces of modern technology that were available; I would have to rely on my clinical acumen. Because of this limited diagnostic capacity, I had to send him down to the local hospital for a more thorough check-up. As was the case with so many of our patients, I never heard back from anyone concerning his case. I never got a referral, nor was I able to track down someone who knew about his case. For a primary care physician, not having follow up was the antithesis of medical practice, as attending the suffering of the sick and infirm was all about follow through.

My worst fear was that I would have to practice obstetrics. I had been trained in general internal medicine and not family medicine, so I had had a modicum of gynecology training and even less obstetrical experience. My fears became manifest when a woman arrived in the ER complaining of recurrent vaginal bleeding after a miscarriage that had occurred 4 weeks before. The recommended course of action would have been a dilation and curettage, to clean out the remnants of tissue in the womb that could cause danger to her health. I had never done one, but fortunately one of the other volunteer doctors with some gynecologic experience was ready to help. Before we could begin, however, the woman decided to leave because she had no childcare at home. It was a good lesson for me early on, that at times social issues play a much larger role in people's decision-making process about their own health than the risks conveyed from their provider. I had dealt with patients' social issues before, having trained at a public hospital in urban Boston/Cambridge, but this was an entirely new context. Refugees living in India, a country with limited resources and a sizeable population living on the brink of starvation, had to struggle just to keep their families alive from week to week.

The next arrival was a 68-year-old man with mild dementia who had already been seen and discharged a few hours earlier. This time, he complained of chest pain. I felt my confidence return, as this had been a common complaint in my residency emergency department, and a problem I felt comfortable treating! In this situation, however, the electrocardiogram didn't work, and the X-ray machine was down for repairs. I examined him thoroughly, diagnosed him as having musculoskeletal pain, and tucked him into the bed in our holding room for the night to help alleviate his anxiety. Luckily the electrocardiogram wasn't necessary, although owing to his age I would have done one in the U.S. to be sure that he didn't have heart disease. At Delek Hospital, we would have to do with what we had. His symptoms seemed to abate suddenly when he saw that I was going to be close by all evening. No sooner had I finished his case than the power went out in the hospital.

Physicians diagnose many things by touch of the human body, but examining patients in the dark presents particular challenges. Often times the "look" of an ill person is all that is needed to identify their specific disease, such as the callow look of a cancer patient, the bronzed skin of a patient with iron overload, or the classic eruptive rash of a child with measles. With the power out, I had essentially lost one of my senses. Luckily, no severe cases showed up at our door that night. Several patients came in with what would become the basis of our practice, gastrointestinal distress and loose stools. Our lab technician, who was "on call" almost every night for severe cases, was able to find the amoeba parasite in their stool samples. By the time I went to sleep, I finally felt that I was on the road to helping a few patients feel better. As I retired back to my room I somehow also knew that my rusty obstetrical skills would be called upon again, sooner rather than later.

Of course, that's exactly what happened. A pregnant woman arrived in labor just before midnight, despite the town being shrouded in darkness. It had been almost 5 years since I had delivered a baby into this world during a medical school obstetrical rotation, but I hadn't brought my medical school notes with me. I was honestly petrified of delivering babies. So I was relieved when one of the British general practice doctors named Kevin agreed to help, despite it being his night off.

The mother was only 20 years old and had just arrived from Tibet. She told us that she had been in labor for almost 36 hours. The tough work of cervical dilation was already over, so all we had to do was coach her through the final stage of pushing. The delivery went smoothly. An hour later, the Tibetan refugee community had its newest member, a healthy baby boy. My hopes were with this child, that he would live long enough to see his fellow Tibetans return to a free Tibet one day.

After the baby arrived, the woman's husband made *tsampa* – roasted barley mixed with butter blessed by a lama – right next to her bed. He took out the roasted grain from a satchel and placed it in a ritual bowl near the mother's bed. A small lit candle provided the heat to melt the butter, which he worked into the grain with a kneading motion of his palm and fingers. Slowly the *tsampa* began to take shape, until he held the dough-like substance in his hand. As it had already been cooked, the food was "ready to eat" for we the honored guests. He graciously gave us each a small portion to eat, so we could share the happy moment with his family. He then fed his wife and newborn son. I felt privileged to watch this intimate ritual take place in our dark and disheveled delivery room. No matter how anxious I was about delivering more babies in the dark, I was grateful for an experience that would stay with me for years to come. It was a soft, peaceful moment, the kind of moment that you can't capture in a medical school lecture. In many ways I too, like this young Tibetan child, had arrived.

2

Settling In

During my first week, we had five more deliveries in 3 days – a record for Delek Hospital as far as anyone could remember. The first three were Tibetan women, who gave birth to girls. The next two were Indian women, who delighted their families by delivering boys. From what I had learned about traditional Indian society, boys are more highly prized than girls are. Girls are thought to cost families money, as they necessitate payment of a dowry and don't necessarily bring a salary into the household. In India sex preference has recently become a medicalized issue, with male sex selected through the use of prenatal ultrasound and selective abortion of females. The practice is illegal, but still occurs in back alleyways. I have heard that in some regions of India there are 5% fewer girls than boys because of this practice.

In contrast, during different periods of Tibetan history, their society had been matrilineal, and women had inherited land and made major family decisions. It was not uncommon for a woman to have two husbands. I wasn't sure if this was still the case. My impression was that in exile in India, Tibetan boys seemed to be more highly valued.

"It's so upsetting," I said to Nyima, one of the allopathically trained Tibetan doctors, "that boys are prized and girls are a disappointment."

"These families took it well," Nyima replied. "Once, I had an Indian mother beg me to kill her baby, after she gave birth to her third daughter. Her family had threatened to kill her if she didn't produce a male offspring."

Despite these daily culture shocks, it didn't take me long to settle into my new home. Some adjustments were more difficult than others. Twelve of us shared one bathroom that had a squat toilet, something I never got used to. At least it was possible to take a warm shower. This required placing a coil heater into a bucket of water. Once it was warm, you used a scooper to pour the water over your head and body. It was not the most efficient way to wash, but I got used to small adjustments like this while living a simpler life. Corporal maintenance needs to be flexible in these situations!

Meals tended to be lively communal affairs on the roof deck overlooking the plains. At any one time, there would be 4 to 5 volunteers from the U.S., Britain, and Australia staffing the hospital, and meal preparation was the time we spent together to decompress from the day. We cooked three or four dinners together every week, using a small gas stove provided by the hospital. Because we had no refrigerator and could not store meat, our mainstay became vegetable stir-fry with rice. Dharamsala's market, Kotwali Bazaar, was just a short walk down the hill and sold everything from vegetables to non-stick skillets, from televisions to toilet paper (no floral designs, though.) The market did not have smoked salmon or good wine, however, both of which I missed. It didn't take me long to drink my last mini-bottle of red wine from the Air France flight to Delhi. Italian spices were largely absent from the market. Knowing of my culinary plight my mother and grandmother sent "care" packages which included oregano and basil for making homemade pasta sauce.

Several times a week, we ate out at one of the Tibetan restaurants. They tended to serve oily noodle soups with questionable ground-up meat bits, as well as tasty dumplings called *momos.* For desert, we indulged in the scrumptious chocolate cake at a small Sikh-owned café called the Chocolate Log. It was in a secluded forest area – a wonderful place to sit and relax when we had time.

Of course, relaxing and eating chocolate cake accounted for a very small percentage of my time. Within my first couple of weeks in Dharamsala, my schedule was quite full: hospital ward coverage, outpatient clinic, Tibetan lessons with a disorganized nun, and hospital ward coverage all over again. I had hoped to spend at least a third of my time on some type of public health project, but with 65 hours of hospital and clinic time per week, the likelihood of doing much else disappeared.

I might have felt confined within the hospital walls, if it were not for the frequent visits to satellite clinics. I was happy to venture to the community health center, the best substitute for house calls that we had. My first trip took me to the McLeod Ganj Community Health Center in upper Dharamsala. McLeod Ganj is the small "neighborhood" on top of the hill above Dharamsala, where most of the area's Tibetans live. In fact, it functions as its own town (one could spend all one's time in lower Dharamsala and never see a Tibetan). On the climb up, I passed the modest but spacious residence compound of the fourteenth Dalai Lama of Tibet, Tenzin Gyatso. The compound was just 400 yards uphill from Delek Hospital, in an area thick with tall conifers and lumpy rhododendrons reminiscent of a Dr. Seuss book illustration. Tibetans of all ages spun prayer wheels and walked clock-wise along the *lingkor*, or holy path, that encircled the home of their spiritual leader. I followed the path for about 10 minutes and came to Namgyal, the ridge-top monastery of the Dalai Lama. The structure was simple and not overly ornate as some Tibetan temples can be, but the courtyard could hold thousands during ceremonies or the public audiences given by the Dalai Lama. The monastery was home to about 180 monks, some practicing the art of debate (*riglam*, literally "mind path" in Tibetan) in the courtyard. While one partner sat on the floor to studiously listen to and critique the other, the debater would slap his hands in a smooth motion with one arm finishing extended. The debaters repeated the motion over and over again towards their debating partners to emphasize their verbal arguments (*thaksel*, for "reasoning one's thesis"). They wore intense facial expressions like graduate students defending their theses. The courtyard with filled with a cacophony of slaps and chants.

Continuing along the ridge past several resort hotels, I reached McLeod Ganj at 5900 feet above sea level. Once an English hill station (resort), the community was now a Tibetan settlement and monastic retreat. Most of the refugees lived in brick homes, their tin roofs waterproofed with plastic sheets held down by rocks. The three main streets offered a wide selection of Indian and Tibetan restaurants, plus several catering to travelers, with promises of Western-style pancakes, omelets, and spaghetti.

I found the McLeod Ganj Community Health Center in the same building as the Tibetan Women's Association. Outside, an old woman stood praying, spinning her Tibetan prayer wheel. The health center had just three rooms and a small pharmacy. There were two Tibetan nurses, Choeden and Youdon, both of whom who spoke excellent English, and an English volunteer named Betsy.

"We see a lot of travelers with diarrhea," Betsy told me. "They come up here to study Buddhist meditation and end up with a nasty case of *E. coli,* giardia, or if they're really unlucky, amoebic dysentery. I've even seen a few cases of typhoid. Oh, and at the moment, the Tushita Retreat Center is having a hepatitis outbreak. I guess the rigorous meditation schedule doesn't include time for washing your hands." I wasn't surprised at what she told me. Westerners traveling to places with different bacteria in the food and water often get sick with what is popularly known as the "Delhi belly," whether you travel through Mexico, Egypt, or India. But I found it a bit ironic to travel all this way to the Tibetan refugee community and end up treating a foreigner's gastrointestinal distress.

In addition to treating unlucky Westerners, I examined many Tibetan children during my first day in McLeod Ganj. Pediatrics was not my specialty, so I was thankful most only had colds or mild diarrhea. Because the health center had no lab, we sent the sickest patients down to Delek Hospital for the few blood tests available there. The center also had an X-ray machine available, although we limited the number of X-rays we took because the film was hard to come by. This was the second irony of the day, that I was trained to be an adult medicine specialist, an internist, but I was plunged head-first into the practice of family medicine of all kinds. I would have to adjust to the new circumstances. This was appropriate anyway, as I am a firm believer in primary care and the concept that one physician should be able to manage the physical and mental health of an entire family, rare diseases not withstanding.

While most of the children were brought in by their mothers, a few came from the nearby Tibetan Children's Village (TCV). At the moment, 2,400 Tibetan children were living and studying at TCV, a large and crowded boarding school supported by international donors, where each child had a sponsor. The Dalai Lama's sister, Jetsun Pema, ran the school. Parents dropped their children off, then returned to Tibet or their adopted homes in India, hoping their children would learn more of the Tibetan language and culture than was possible under Chinese rule in their homeland. Many of the young staff in the Tibetan Government-in-Exile began their education at TCV and went on to Indian universities.

After finishing up at the health center, I was lucky enough to watch the TCV team defeat McLeod Team B in the Tibetan soccer final. Monks in burgundy robes cheered the teams on, waving flags and shouting from the stands. The game was punctuated by the straying of large, brown cows onto the field of play. They were unconcerned about our game. These lugubrious cows, who intermittently wandered across the length of the field, seemed oblivious to the enormity of the event they were disturbing. Of course, in India, cows are considered sacred and are treated as holy creatures, so they could not be chased off the field. The locals also take time to wash these creatures, leading me to think that improving hygienic practices in the community would not be impossible.

During my next call day at the hospital, a mother brought in her young child, limp and unable to move. Based on the mother's history of her daughter's symptoms, I quickly diagnosed her with cerebral meningitis and knew that the only chance we had to save her was getting her intravenous treatment with the few antibiotics we had. I was unsuccessful. We were able to thread a plastic catheter into her collapsed veins, but she soon stopped breathing. I knew it was hopeless to try any extraordinary measures to bring her back.

Moments after the child died, an older patient went into cardiac arrest, and Chokyi, our nurse aide, had no idea what to do. Cardiac arrest was just not something that commonly happened there. It took several minutes to get an oxygen tank hooked up and administer an epinephrine shot into his buttocks. The man had no pulse for what seemed like an eternity. I was about to give him a "cardiac thump" worth about 50 joules of energy to get his heart reset to zero, when he spontaneously woke up. He didn't remember a thing, and was curious why all of us were standing next to his bed. The standard treatment in the West would be to run some blood tests to check for a heart attack, and keep him monitored for 24 hours to make sure it didn't happen again. Our EKG didn't work, however, and we could not order the standard blood tests, so for the moment there was nothing more we could do for him other than intermittently check his pulse (which was well accepted as this was the method traditional Tibetan doctors use). Both cases reminded me of how delicate a balance life can really be.

Of the seven admissions that day, one appeared to be a case of cholera. Without a proper lab, it was impossible to be sure. The inability to confirm a diagnosis constantly forced us to use more antibiotics than necessary, no doubt contributing to drug resistance. This problem was probably made worse by the fact that anyone could go down to the market and buy any drug without a prescription. We chose to treat him with oral and intravenous fluids, and save the antibiotics for when he would really need them. It was the right choice, as he was able to recover quickly.

That evening, just before dinner, we admitted a man with TB and emphysema. The X-ray of his lungs looked like Swiss cheese. It showed that he probably had only a few remaining air pockets for the exchange of oxygen. The TB ward was full, so we had to shift some patients around to squeeze him in. The nearest ventilator was 4 hours away, and we had no way to treat such badly diseased lungs.

"Can we get him some oxygen somehow?" I said desperately.

"There's no way to get compressed air up here. There are no companies that service this area regularly," Dr. Tsetan told me.

My frustration rose with each passing minute, as I watched him gasp for each successive breath. I felt so impotent; as a trained physician I knew exactly what this man needed to stay alive, but I lacked the tools with which to do it. It was near agony to watch him struggle with air hunger, and to watch him die from lack of access to oxygen. When he expired late that evening, I think we were all relieved that his suffering was finally over. I exchanged a few words with a Buddhist monk who had come to attend to the family about the finality of death and the impermanence of life, and then went upstairs to rest, physically spent.

The weather worsened before midnight, starting first as light rain but quickly changing to another monsoon-style downpour. I fell asleep from mental and spiritual exhaustion. When the howling wind and crackling thunder woke me up later that night, I was convinced I was back in Iowa, listening to a Midwestern-style thunderstorm, complete with the roof-shattering lightning and thunder that I had heard so often in childhood. But the dawn revealed I was still at the foot of the Himalayas, in my tiny room with the magnificent view. Watching the morning light roll over the hills and valleys, it was impossible to imagine what the day was going to bring.

As it turned out, it brought three dozen patients in the first 5 hours of my shift, including two new cases of TB. One was a young woman, who looked perfectly fine until she started coughing up blood right in our waiting area. TB is so common in the Tibetan community that they call it *"Tibetan birmar"* in Hindi, or "Tibetan disease." For those unfamiliar with this millennia-old plague of humanity, tuberculosis is caused by bacteria that spread from person to person through infected respiratory droplets that are coughed out and then remain suspended in the air. The bacteria are inhaled by another person, settle in the lungs of the uninfected person and begin to multiply, often very slowly. From there, the infection can move through the blood to other parts of the body, including the spine and brain. While it was once the leading cause of death in the United States, TB is now completely curable in areas with proper medical care and access to the right medicine. Despite this, it remains the second leading cause of death from infectious diseases worldwide, killing an estimated 1.7 million people each year. The problem for the developing world is that sick patients may go weeks or months before seeing a doctor. This gives them the chance to spread the infection to those persons near them or in contact with them with every cough or sneeze. When these ill patients are finally diagnosed, the advanced stage of the disease makes it that much tougher to treat. The extent of the problem at Delek Hospital was obvious from the vast portion of resources devoted to diagnosing and treating TB. The ward for persons with TB took up roughly a quarter of the hospital building and was always full.

Aside from ward coverage and satellite clinics, my duties included weekly visits to the Elders Home, just below the Dalai Lama's residence. The building housed 75 elderly Tibetans with weathered faces and stooped walks. The hospital did not have enough resources to fund regular nursing staff to assist the residents or hand out medications. The prayer hall full of musty *thangka* paintings doubled as a clinic, with patients kneeling on the floor as they waited their turn. During my first visit, I saw about 20 men and women with the assistance of an interpreter who spoke broken English. As best I could tell, most of the patients suffered from diabetes, hypertension, or arthritis, the same chronic illnesses that plague industrialized society. Diabetes and hypertension are diseases that manifest quietly; the sufferer doesn't necessarily know he or she is afflicted and therefore is not often motivated to continue taking medication long term. I could tell from the medical chart notes by the physicians who had come before me, that they were stuck between a rock and a hard place: patients that didn't feel the need to take their medication daily, and the challenges of having medication stocked in the hospital pharmacy. Arthritis pain was another matter. Every single elder seemed to complain of this ache or that ache, and were all too happy to take any pain medication we had to offer.

Before I left, the interpreter led me down a dark hallway to do a "room call." I found a withered man in dirty clothes. From what I was able to discern, the man hadn't urinated in a whole week, and there were no catheters for a nurse or doctor to insert to empty his bladder. I arranged to get him to the hospital to get a catheter inserted, and to have someone check for enlargement of the prostate, or worse, prostate cancer. Even a small problem like an enlarged prostate could, in our context, be life threatening if he wasn't able to urinate. The resulting "backup" of urine could cause kidney failure and death. As I walked back down the hill, I wondered how many other critical patients might be tucked away in the corners of the Elders Home, actually a nursing home without nurses.

Back at the hospital, two young men carried in an elder Tibetan whose abdomen was swollen with fluid. I took one look at the man and saw all the classic physical signs of chronic alcoholic liver disease. He had the rosy cheeks, oversized nose, and belly full of fluid typical of someone who has taken one too many drinks in his lifetime. A quick discussion with his son-in-law revealed the elder's drink of choice was homemade *chang*, a Tibetan brew made with millet. I had seen fluid buildup in the abdomen (ascites) from alcoholic liver disease hundreds of times back in the U.S. and felt confident prescribing bed rest, salt restriction, and a few rounds of intravenous diuretics. I felt satisfied that this one patient's acute problem I could treat.

Next, I turned my attention to a young boy with vomiting and diarrhea. He could have had anything, but his problem became obvious when he vomited up a thin, foot-long intestinal worm into his bedside pail. I was pretty sure by the look of it that is was *Ascaris lumbridoides*, a very common intestinal infection in India. If left untreated, the worms take nutrients away from growing children, causing stunting and growth retardation. If they grow too large, they can actually cause intestinal obstruction. It wasn't the most pleasant sight, to see this boy vomiting up such a large parasite, but it was good to know that his body was rejecting it. It's an infection that is easily cured with one dose of anti-worm medicine, but unsettling none the same.

The most eventful case of the day was a young nun in her 20s with a large gash in her upper arm.

"*Tashi delek*," I said, a universal greeting that means "Auspicious greetings to you" or "Good health to you" in Tibetan.

"*Tashi delek.*" she said while wincing. "I was trying to help a mule," she explained through our translator. "Its reins were all tangled up in a bush. When I tried to set it free, it got frightened and bit my arm."

The mule's teeth had obviously penetrated the nun's biceps. Although I didn't have much experience stitching up deep wounds, I managed to close the entire gash.

She looked incredulously at the row of stitches and then up at me. "I never knew it was possible to sew up a person's arm as if it were a torn cotton shirt!"

I too was proud of my "tailoring," until the next day when it became obvious the wound was infected. This necessitated opening up the top layer to let the infection drain. It had been a mistake for me to sew the gash up completely. 1 should have anticipated the possibility of infection, considering a dirty-mouthed beast had deeply bitten a human arm. This was a hard lesson for me to learn, and an embarrassing one, but one that would serve me well in all the future episodes of suturing wounds in the coming year. As for the nun, it seemed that it was not a big deal to her at all, so I tried not to make it one for me.

The important issue was whether or not to give the nun rabies vaccine. The only variety available required a series of six shots over 90 days. I had never heard of a mule with rabies. It seemed awfully unlikely. But after consulting with the other doctors, we decided to go with the doctrine of "better safe than sorry." We started her on the series of rabies vaccine injections, which she dutifully took without missing a single one. It cost the hospital a fair amount of money, but we were confident it had been the correct course of action.

Meanwhile, my alcoholic patient failed to improve on the conservative regimen I had prescribed. He remained in considerable discomfort, and I decided to resort to more drastic measures to get the fluid out of his abdomen. First, I sent his son-in-law to the city of Pathankot in Punjab, 4 hours away, to find some human albumin. When he returned, I drained 2.5 liters of ascites from the man's abdomen, while infusing his veins with the albumin. I was astonished to learn the albumin cost the equivalent of two months' wages for a nurse, and the son-in-law had paid this. I felt reluctant to ask the son about the cost. I vowed that I would think harder the next time about passing the cost of practicing modern medicine in a developing country onto the poor. In the best of all possible worlds, the health care system would have paid for this drug. Delek Hospital, however, did not have the funds with which to purchase expensive medications. It was a luxury we had to do without.

That evening, the sunset from the hospital roof deck was a perfect mixture of translucent oranges, pale blue, and fuchsia. The sun tended to make dramatic exits throughout monsoon season, which offered some compensation for the fact that the days were filled with torrential downpours. It rained so much that our papers were damp, our clothes were damp, our leather shoes were covered in mildew, and our towels never quite dried out. However, the end of the season was overdue, and my spirit soared when I awoke to clear skies the next morning.

It was the day of His Holiness the Dalai Lama's return from a trip to Mongolia and England. I was examining a woman with presumed rheumatoid arthritis when I heard the warning truck go by.

"Do you mind if we continue this outside?" I asked her. I didn't want to miss the motorcade. She duly consented with a quick nod and raced outside herself.

The street was filled with Tibetans holding flowers and clumps of burning incense. Most wore expressions of awe and bowed deeply as their spiritual leader passed. Waves of "*Tashi delek*" rose from the crowd. Once the motorcade was out of sight, the devotees headed home smiling, and I headed inside to a backlog of waiting but contented patients. Any opportunity for Tibetans to see His Holiness the Dalai Lama in public is a happy one.

My next call day brought another frightful labor and delivery. The last thing I wanted was a complicated labor, but a 17-year-old Tibetan girl was about to give me just that. She had burst her membranes some time earlier and had pus faintly oozing out of her vagina. The fetal heartbeat seemed stable, but the baby failed to progress through the uterus during the second stage of labor. She didn't seem to understand the need to push, and the baby got stuck in the birth canal. That's when I called in the troops.

"Maybe we should show her the forceps as an incentive," Kevin, one of the other volunteers, suggested.

I frowned at him. "That seems a bit harsh on my scale. Aren't forceps associated with damage to the skull in some cases?"

"I don't intend to use them, just to show them to her," he said flatly.

While we were debating the idea, Youdon the Tibetan nurse-midwife made the episiotomy a bit larger and pulled the head out herself, obviating the need for our Western mechanics. The baby had all the good predictors of good survival at the beginning, but then failed to breastfeed by the second day. Because we had no idea how long ago the mother's water had broken, we felt the baby was vulnerable to infection and started her on antibiotics. After several days the baby suddenly became brighter, and began to breastfeed spontaneously. Although we didn't know what we had treated, our intervention had probably saved the baby's life.

What a relief when my next patient turned out to be a *Rinpoche*, or reincarnated lama, with chronic back and neck pain.

"When you meditate, do you maintain the same seated position for hours at a time?" I asked.

He looked at me as if I were from Mars. "Of course we sit, it's our daily practice."

"That puts a strain on your back. Changing positions would help. Maybe you could try lying down when you meditate or chant?"

Everyone in the room burst out laughing, including the lama. "I'd fall asleep if I tried that! Chanting is not all that interesting!" Tibetans have a wonderful manner of laughter, jolly, good natured and impish at times. I ended up laughing at myself.

Now the truth was out, and straight from the mouth of a *Rinpoche!* I ended up prescribing him some anti-inflammatory medication, which he took dutifully. I also suggested that he take some Tibetan medicine, as allopathic (Western) medicine does not have very effective medications for treating chronic pain.

Traditional Tibetan society has a multilayered medical system. This ranges from local, community-led shamanic and folk Buddhist ritual practitioners and practices, to religious and secular practitioners of a scholarly tradition of health care rooted in the naturalistic ethnomedical medical paradigms of the Middle East, Asia, and Europe. The Buddhist notion of mind or self, emotion, and the law of karma, is based on a theoretical system in which the notion of mental self is constituted as dominant over the objective, or grossly physical body. The etiology of disease can be, according to classical teaching, reduced to an understanding of the "Noble Truths." Namely, that life is impermanent, and that impermanence leads to suffering through the operations or attachments of the ego, or self. Ego is manifested in the forms of delusion, ignorance, and confusion. These, in turn, give rise to attachment, greed, desire, hatred, aversion, and aggression. Traditional Tibetan (Buddhist) medicine posits that the self (ego) is ultimately the cause of all suffering, including that of ill health. Although body and mind are seen to be fundamentally integrated into one system, it is the mind that is problematized and seen as primary in facilitating both health and ill health. In contrast to allopathic medicine, where the mind is treated as a component of the physical body, in classical Buddhist medical theory the physical body is subsumed conceptually into the mind.

The goal of traditional Tibetan medical practice is the maintenance and restoration of the delicate balance of the *Nyipa sum*, the three fundamental humors that underlie all body functions and health. These humors, also the cause of afflictions, are air (*rLung*), bile (*mKhris-pa*), and phlegm (*Bad-kan*). These do not correspond to the Western views of air (life-sustaining oxygen), bile (liver substance to release toxins), and phlegm (mucus to protect the body). To the contrary, the humors are linked to the fundamental elements of material existence: earth, water, fire, air, and space. Translated to the patient level, this involves examination of an individual's disorder in relationship to climate, time, diet, and behavior. It takes years of practice to become a skilled Tibetan physician.

The next afternoon was filled with routine physicals on newly arrived teenagers. Many had fled Tibet in small groups, by walking over the mountains into Nepal. One boy had lost all the toes on his right foot to frostbite. I wished I had more time to spend with the teens. By discussing basic hygiene and nutrition, I could have made a far greater difference in their lives. Health education was my specialty, but instead, I was obliged to be on duty in the hospital treating dehydration and sewing up wounds. Though my schedule was tight, I still hoped to find a way to make a more lasting contribution to the health of the community.

Dharamsala, and the Tibetan neighborhood of McLeod Ganj above it, rest in the foothills of the Dhalaudar Range in the Himalayan Mountains of India.

Delek Hospital during a mid-winter snowstorm.

Sogar Transit School for new arrivals is located in the lower plains below Dharamsala.

Delivering community health messages at Sogar School was a routine part of serving as a Delek Hospital physician.

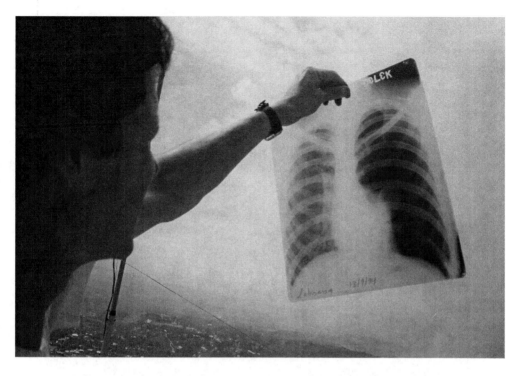

Chest X-rays often had to be read by holding them up to the sky.

A typical medicine cabinet in the outlying Tibetan settlements had just a few basic essential medicines available for distribution.

3

Taking On the Tough Issues

A day in Delek Hospital's outpatient department was a test of stamina for both the doctors and patients. Though the official clinic hours were from 9:15 a.m. until 12:30 p.m., in reality the day began much earlier, and the clinic closed much later. Jeeps full of refugees from nearby settlements began arriving at 7 a.m., which for them meant they had left their villages by 5 a.m. or earlier. Indian patients from McLeod Ganj, Dharamsala, and surrounding villages had less far to travel, but they still had to show up early to get a place in line. By 8:30 a.m., the sick, injured, and worried had crammed themselves into the waiting area, a large balcony just outside the exam room. There was no official line, but everyone seemed to know who was next. Surprisingly, despite being ill and having to wait for hours, the patients were always cordial, and fights never broke out in the waiting area.

The patient population was predominantly Tibetan, from the nearby town as well as from more distant settlements. Local Indian herders from the Gadi tribe who spoke Hindi also occasionally came to see us, as it was more convenient for them to pay a small fee to be seen by Western physicians, rather than wait in the overcrowded and chaotic Indian hospital in the main town and be seen for free. Western tourists also took advantage of our services; in fact, at times it seemed to us that they were the majority of our patients. They were the ones to easily fall prey to the various ailments common in the Indian subcontinent. Despite drinking only bottled water, and eating only cooked food rather than snacks like raw vegetables, it was only a matter of time before a visiting Westerner came down with watery diarrhea, or even worse, dysentery (diarrhea with blood).

Owing to the large number of patients packed into the clinic, patient confidentiality was often the first precept of the practice of medicine to be compromised. Those waiting on the balcony could watch everything through a window and sometimes wandered into the exam room to get a closer look. This was the first aspect of clinical practice in the outpatient clinic that I had a hard time getting used to. I can handle having rudimentary instruments at my disposal, but to have a complete stranger looking over my shoulder as I talk to a patient about sensitive topics like menstrual periods or bowel movements goes against a basic principle of medicine we are taught in the West – privacy and confidentiality. I tried to maintain as private a space as possible, but inevitably in one corner of our large exam rooms there was some other activity going on, from cleaning a wound in the sink to explaining something to another patient's family. In a sense, I began to learn that in a small community, there really is no such thing as privacy.

The workload was also an adjustment at first, as I was not used to such a heavy volume of patients. My usual caseload in my Cambridge residency had been eight patients in one 3-hour session. The Delek Hospital expected you to see that many in less than one hour. After several months, I could usually see two or three dozen patients before lunch, including Tibetan officials who arrived late and sneaked to the front of the line. Once, my first patient was the assistant head of the Tibetan Medical and Astrological Institute (*Men Tsee Khang* in Tibetan). This man was an expert in Tibetan medicine, yet there he was in our clinic with no more than a cold – something I thought Tibetan medicine was better equipped to handle! I enjoyed the fact that traditional Tibetan physicians trusted our skills enough to come in for an evaluation. Moreover, I think one or two of us allopathic physicians visited the traditional Tibetan medicine clinic throughout the year—yet we likely did not put traditional medicine ahead of Western pharmacology in our own medicine cabinets.

For non-VIP's, the day began with a long wait, followed by a short visit with one of the doctors, then lab tests if necessary. These tests usually cost twice as much as seeing the doctor and necessitated waiting several hours for results. The fees were supposed to help keep down the patient load, but we saw so many people with minor problems I couldn't imagine more coming if the clinic were free. In my view, the fees had the potential to keep away the poorest Tibetans even if they were seriously ill, but didn't deter the rest no matter how small their complaints. I could hardly believe how many people waited in clinic all day long because of colds, headaches, or other minor ailments that my grandmother could have treated. They came in for a variety of reasons, such as a need for reassurance, validation of their illness, or a "laying on of hands." No matter where you practice, the "worried well" (those who are physically well, just more worried than sick) are part of your everyday routine. And once in a while, one of those minor ailments turns out to be that rare zebra you've always dreaded finding.

One nice thing about the clinic, from a doctor's point of view, was that the patients carried their own medical records. Of course, everyone seemed to roll their X-rays, fold them, or stuff them into some type of small container, which made them rather tough to read. But it did save time, since we didn't have to dig through clinic records, and saving time was a high priority when the average patient load was eight people an hour. That meant completing the interview, exam, diagnosis, recommendations, and note writing in 6 or 7 minutes per patient.

The nursing aides who acted as interpreters frequently sent me non-verbal cues if I spent too much time with one patient. They seemed to think a diagnosis could be made in 30 seconds flat with a minimal physical exam, and they discouraged me from asking too many questions. It was all in good faith, as they had a responsibility to be sure that all the patients were seen. I tried to explain that it was impossible to practice good medicine with so little time to analyze each problem, even if someone just had a common cold. Sure, you could find out that a patient had diarrhea, check for dehydration, and prescribe broad-spectrum antibiotics in just a few minutes, but you learned nothing about his or her past history or the underlying cause of the illness. I felt that the clinic's assembly-line atmosphere prevented me from establishing a rapport with the patients and, in some cases, limited the effectiveness of the treatments we offered. I dare say this is the standard in most parts of the developing world where the patient-physician ratio is extremely high.

Nowhere was our time crunch more evident than with patients who showed signs of mental illness. Among those with mental health problems, depression was the most common clinical diagnosis we made. I diagnosed at least two patients with depression every week, but never had the chance to get to know the person well. In the interest of timeliness, the nursing aides always suggested the same solution: give them an antidepressant and send them on their un-merry way. Psychotherapy was not part of the therapeutic equation, especially not when 30 people are waiting to see you. We ended up seeing these patients on our own time, after clinic hours, which most of the time was a pleasure.

Once a well-dressed Tibetan woman from McLeod Ganj came to the clinic complaining that she didn't feel well, that she wasn't hungry. I suspected clinical depression and started asking some questions about her background.

"There's no time for this," Chokyi my aide gently hinted.

I became firm. "Please translate her answers for me. I want to get to know her better. I truly believe we can help people with these symptoms not by giving drugs, but by listening." The aide reluctantly did as I asked. I learned that the patient was divorced and short of money. Her children had left home. Her only source of income – teaching Tibetan to a foreigner – was about to dry up. As she revealed all this, she started to cry. The aide's eyes grew big. Apparently, she hadn't expected this from a seemingly proud middle-aged Tibetan woman. Tibetans are known to hold their emotions close to their hearts. I felt a tinge of inner satisfaction. I knew we were opening up new places for her.

I talked with the patient a little longer and made plans for a follow-up visit. When her lab tests came back normal as expected, I tried discussing how we could best treat her depression. The concept of psychotherapy hadn't taken hold yet in the Tibetan community, because Tibetans felt the lamas could fill the role of counselor when needed. Therefore, the woman opted for nothing, but seemed to look better. Over the following weeks, she smiled whenever we passed each other in the streets. I often wonder how she is doing, many years after this encounter.

It was no mystery to me why so many of the Tibetans I met suffered from depression. One can find mental health disturbances in any refugee population that has undergone stress. Many Tibetans had been separated from their homeland for more than three decades with little hope of ever returning. Others were newly arrived nuns or monks with no family or possessions, just vivid memories of being arrested by the Chinese, imprisoned, and sometimes tortured before being released and fleeing Tibet. One man I interviewed during clinic one day vividly described standing on a wet floor while the Chinese poked him with electric cattle prods.

When I arrived, Dharamsala had no special clinic for these torture survivors, and Delek Hospital had neither the time nor the resources to properly treat post-traumatic stress disorder, anxiety, or depression, let alone full-blown psychosis. Several European organizations had funded the creation of a program for torture victims housed within the Ministry of Health that could eventually fill this void. In the meantime, many refugees kept their pasts to themselves and lived in a state of perpetual anguish. Even those who were deeply disturbed had little hope of receiving adequate care.

Such was the case when guards from the Department of Security brought in a psychotic monk. The young man, recently arrived from Tibet, had been exhibiting bizarre behavior in his settlement.

"What type of behavior?" I asked.

"Mumbling Chinese in the streets and taking apart electrical fuse boxes on people's houses," one of the guards told me. "Some of the other settlers got very angry with him. They beat him up and left him in a gutter. That's when we decided to bring him here."

The monk spent the next few days throwing food and peeing on other patients' beds. He eventually calmed down, though not before I gave him a good dose of the anti-psychotic drug haloperidol. My differential diagnosis focused on possible schizophrenia or acute psychosis (a mental disorder in which one loses contact with reality, such as hearing voices or having delusions that someone is out to get you), which was confirmed by the Indian psychiatrist in town, who did not routinely treat Tibetans. A few days later, the monk escaped while his guards were playing cards on the hospital's porch. Who knows where he ended up – or whose electrical circuits he managed to alter without their knowledge.

As if one psychotic monk weren't enough to handle in a hospital with absolutely no psychiatric services, a second monk with similar symptoms showed up a few days later. This one was middle-aged and had no past history of mental illness. But now he had florid psychosis (had lost contact with reality): he was convinced that his monastery's gardener and the Indian army were out to get him and that the other monks were jealous of his room. He vividly described Chinese army bombs dropping on his roof, something probably never seen in Dharamsala. When he was brought to the hospital, it wasn't too hard to see that he was having serious paranoid delusions (thinking something that is not true) and hallucinations (seeing something not really there). What to do next? We put him in the ward reserved for people suspected of having TB, and now, psychotic people. After several days on the only drug we had for psychosis, he settled down a bit. After this episode, I urged the hospital director to look into hiring someone in the field of mental health. We were told that there was not a single Tibetan psychiatrist in all of India, so getting a culturally appropriate treatment team together to manage mental health problems seemed like a far-fetched goal. There also was probably not a large enough demand for a full time provider, so we were left with a patchwork quilt of coverage.

Over the next few months, we heard that the Torture Survivors Program was finally up and running, but with only one paid staff person and no full time psychologist or medical professional. The program was relying on sporadic visits by foreign psychiatrists, which was not a sustainable model of care. To their credit, however, the program was offering free housing and social support for those that enrolled. In the face of hundreds of Tibetans needing evaluation, however, the number of enrollees was only in the single digits.

My next call day shifted my attention from mental health to meningitis, an infection of the thin outer covering of the brain. It is usually from bacteria but can be from a virus. A 25-year-old monk from the Dalai Lama's monastery was brought in nearly unconscious by his fellow monks. Tenzin had been under the care of the Tibetan Medical and Astrological Institute for the past 2 days, but had started to weave in and out of consciousness and was complaining of a stiff neck. I immediately suspected meningitis and wished he had been brought in sooner. Prompt administration of antibiotics for the most common kinds of bacterial meningitis can often mean the difference between life and death. While Tibetan medicine can successfully treat many conditions, as far as I knew, meningitis was not one of them. Now this young man had arrived in our hospital near death's door.

Knowing meningitis could kill in a matter of hours, I started Tenzin on antibiotics without waiting for all the tests we needed. Luckily I was able to do a spinal tap (sampling of the fluid around the spinal cord and brain, usually taken from the lower back to avoid hitting any nerves) without any trouble, as he was barely conscious. I also requested an X-ray and was shocked when one of the nurses told him to walk to the X-ray room himself. He could barely stand up, let alone walk anywhere, so his friends ended up carrying him. Eventually the lab results suggested I was half-right: Tenzin had TB meningitis, leaving me uncertain as to how best to treat him. I decided to play it safe and gave him all four TB medicines, plus several for regular meningitis. Meanwhile, an entire squadron of monks chanted Tibetan Buddhist mantras in his room. His teacher suggested moving him to the nearest university hospital, 6 hours away in Chandigarh, Punjab. I advised him that we had all the proper medications at Delek and were doing everything we could. At midnight, Tenzin responded to neither voice nor touch, and I let the high lama from Namgyal Monastery know that he might not make it through the rest of the night.

Nevertheless, he survived. The following day found Tenzin much improved, and I was able to leave him long enough to make another house call to the Elders Home, which I had been avoiding. It was not my lovely geriatric patients that troubled me; rather it was the clinical setting. The equipment was in poor condition, the translator barely spoke English, the housing was quite dirty, and there was no health worker to assist the elders with my recommendations. I frequently doubted whether the medicines I prescribed even made it to the right people.

Follow-up visits with three patients with hypertension did little to ease my concerns that day. Wangduk was off all his medications. Mrs. Pema was taking her medicine, but had the timing mixed up. Instead of one dose three times a day, she was taking three pills together every morning. Sangye had run out of his medication a week ago and was too sick to go anywhere for a refill. Most of these problems could have been fixed by a regularly employed community health worker, someone to help keep the patients on track. I decided to write to the Home Department, the office in charge of the facility, to explain the need for improvements and more funds to hire a full-time staff person.

My next couple of visits to outlying refugee communities highlighted another common but fixable problem: nonpotable or unclean, bad drinking water. Sogar Transit School was a small, sparsely furnished encampment in the plains below the hospital, 20 minutes away by car. On a clear day, you could see the tin huts from the hospital roof. Those huts housed about 200 refugees, mostly young men fresh out of Tibet with no jobs and few skills save farming. I was curious to see the settlement for myself, because scores of these men and several women had been up to the hospital complaining of diarrhea.

When I arrived, I was welcomed by a community health worker named Lobsang. He invited me to share some tea, so we had a chance to talk before seeing patients.

"Where does the settlement get its water?" I finally asked.

"From a stream. It's no good during the rainy season, but now that the monsoons are over, it's safe to drink."

"Are you sure?" I asked, a bit incredulous.

I was shocked that he was telling everyone it was safe to drink this untreated water without boiling. No wonder so many of the Sogar School settlers were getting sick. It seemed some health education was in order, for the health worker as well as the settlers. Lobsang had wanted to hold health education classes, but never had any time.

After we finished our tea, the patients lined up outside and inside a small hut that served as a clinic. Most had diarrhea, of course. There was little privacy and only a few basic medicines. I sent those patients with fevers, dehydration, or possible typhoid fever to the hospital. My driver showed up before I finished seeing everyone, and I couldn't convince him to come back later. There were still many more patients to see, but I had to stick to schedule. As I rode back to the hospital, I realized they were all in Lobsang's hands now.

I knew that if we pulled together we could all make a difference. Although I am a firm believer in the community health axiom that I had as much to learn from the refugees as they did from me, I crossed my fingers in the hope that Lobsang had learned a few things about infectious diseases carried by non-potable water. I am meticulous enough in the care of my patients to want to do things myself, but this time I had to relinquish the clinic back to the health worker. Next time, I would take a bus so I could work later.

I had another eye-opening experience during my first session at the Norbulingka Clinic. The real Norbulingka Palace was the Dalai Lama's summer palace on the outskirts of Lhasa, in Tibet. It reportedly used to be a beautiful building, ornate, opulent by Tibetan standards, and richly decorated. When the Chinese government tried to capture the Dalai Lama by inviting him (without bodyguards) to an opera in March 1959, he was residing at Norbulingka. He refused to go, suspecting an ambush. On March 10, 30,000 people gathered outside the palace gate, attempting to protect the Dalai Lama from a possible Chinese attack. He stalled for a week, until the first mortar rounds fell into his inner garden at Norbulingka. That night, he decided to flee, accompanied by scores of advisors and his family, disguised as soldiers. Seven hundred Khampa warriors guarded his safe escape, as he passed within 100 yards of the Chinese, shrouded in darkness. Two days later, on March 20, the Chinese People's Liberation Army shelled Norbulingka heavily. Tibetans gathered near the palace from all over Lhasa. The entire city was certain that His Holiness had died, not knowing of his escape across the Himalayas into India. It took more than 3 weeks for the happy news to reach many parts of Tibet.

The Norbulingka complex was rebuilt at the foot of the Dhauladhar Range, about a 20-minute drive from Dharamsala, and solidified the permanence of the entire area settlement as "Little Lhasa." I stared in awe at the grand buildings, the grounds lush with flora and a menagerie of small animals. It was all very inspiring to a novice like me. The buildings were beautifully crafted and well built, an accurate reflection of the real buildings in Lhasa. What a contrast to the dormitory and plastic tents of the nearby nunnery, Dolma Ling, which housed about 100 newly arrived nuns in very basic conditions![5]

These nuns, along with some local artisans, made up the clientele at the Norbulingka Clinic.

The artisans, who were mostly men, wove carpets and made stuffed panda bears at a workshop in the Norbulingka complex. The carpets were beautiful reproductions of traditional Tibetan designs, with very good workmanship. Their health issues, however, stemmed mainly from the lack of proper equipment and less-than-optimal safety standards on the job, with cuts and eye trauma being far too common. The government had spent U.S. $1 million building a palatial structure, but perhaps had not spent as much as they should have on worker safety. Judging by the number of injured workers whom we saw in our clinic, more could have been done to protect the health of the people who worked there.

As for our patients from the nunnery, nearly all of them had diarrhea. This was no surprise, because many Dolma Ling nuns with the same problem were routinely showing up at Delek Hospital. At any given time, they occupied two or three of our 14 general ward beds. Some of the nuns also had severe problems with foot ulcers. I decided I would return another day to talk to the nuns about their attitudes toward drinking water and hygiene. Since so many of them with diarrhea were sleeping in our hospital with an intravenous drip, I felt it was essential to improve their awareness of water-borne illnesses.

---

[5] The nuns have since been adequately housed and taken care of by the Tibetan Nuns Project, based in Seattle, Washington. See the last few pages of the book for their address.

Over the following week, we got hit by a flood of ill nuns. The number of Dolma Ling nuns occupying our hospital beds climbed at an alarming pace. Every other day, we admitted several nuns with diarrhea and dehydration, most often dysentery from a parasite called an "amoeba." The nurses and doctors were getting somewhat discouraged with the steady stream of ill nuns, so I knew they would be receptive when I suggested a site visit to tackle the problem at its source. It reminded me of the traditional public health aphorism, that in addition to rescuing drowning persons with good medical care, one should also head upstream to figure out why they were falling in the river in the first place! We agreed that I would head to Norbulingka in the morning with our newest employee, an enthusiastic young Tibetan-American named Lhamo who had a public health degree.

While getting ready the next morning, I found a scorpion in my cabinet just inches away from my hand. I violated the Buddhist laws of respect for all life and smashed the poisonous rascal with a shoe. The last thing I needed was a scorpion sting, when a camp full of diarrheal nuns was awaiting our help.

When Lhamo and I arrived in Norbulingka, the clinic was already packed with young nuns from Dolma Ling. The plan was to see patients before lunch and provide health education in the afternoon. I almost decided to treat everybody with a broad-spectrum antibiotic for bacterial causes of diarrhea, and a specialized antibiotic drug for the amoeba parasite. However, it turned out that most of the nuns had mild diarrhea and only needed oral rehydration salts.

The other half of the patients had upper back pain. It was more than a few, which made me wonder what kind of rigorous meditation schedule they were undertaking. I got a lot of laughs by demonstrating massage and more giggles when I suggested that they do it for each other. It surprised me that the concept was strange to them, considering that massage is routine at the monasteries in Thailand. The practice of Buddhism in Tibet and Thailand is different, however. Tibetan Buddhism belongs to the Mahayana, or Greater Vehicle, school, whereas Thai Buddhism is Theravada. Mahayana Buddhists believe that they should delay their entry into nirvana to help all earthly beings in their quest for enlightenment. The acceptance of massage in Buddhist temples in Thailand is, however, more of a cultural difference than one of philosophy.

Once we finished seeing patients, we had noodle soup for lunch and toured the new nunnery under construction. I was surprised to see that it was a large complex designed to house 300 nuns. To get to the temporary camp for our education session, we walked 15 minutes through fields, over a stream, and down a dirt road. Finally, we reached a large grassy area filled with nuns practicing debate. The nuns were arranged in pairs under a large, umbrella-like tree set against the foothills of the Himalayas. Half were kneeling opposite their standing debate partners. They all looked and dressed alike, wearing robes of crimson cloth wrapped over a pale red bodice, their heads shaved to a fine stubble. As they rebutted and refuted their partners' philosophical arguments, the nuns who were standing stressed each point with a hand slap toward the other's face, as I had seen the monks doing earlier. Judging from their expressions, they were having fun at their studies.

We took a quick tour of the nuns' dormitory, which housed 105 women in bunk rooms, four per room. There was a large meeting tent outside and a squat toilet, with no water for washing. We decided to investigate the quality of the water supply and found that many of the nuns drank directly from a stream that ran right under the dormitory. The tap that carried water from the village was only on for 3 or 4 hours each day, so they had to resort to alternate measures at other times. We were surprised to see several water filters lying around next to the tap, unused and unfilled. It wasn't hard to determine what the focus of our health education should be.

After we finished our tour, we gathered 60 nuns under the big tree outside and split them into groups. We gave each group a question, our goal being to find out their basic health knowledge. In contrast to what we expected, they knew quite a lot.

"What behaviors cause illness?" we asked.

Their response: "Not brushing teeth, not washing hands, bad water, not cleaning nails, and coughing into people's faces."

"What behaviors cause diarrhea?"

"Eating old meat, bad water, sour food, and sitting on wet grass."

While some of the nuns seemed more knowledgeable than others, the discussion encouraged them to teach each other, and they seemed to enjoy the process. Their knowledge of basic nutrition was encouraging. One nun eloquently explained the importance of eating green vegetables for iron and vitamins. Knowledge doesn't always translate to practice, however. The nuns' regular diet, something that was probably out of their control, consisted mainly of rice and potatoes.

Next, we gave each nun a glass of water without revealing where the water had come from. All the glasses were clear, even one filled with stream water, which we knew was likely crawling with amoeba. We had a grand time debating where each water sample came from and how it's impossible to tell if the water is safe just by looking. Then I held a glass of stream water, behind my back with some mineral water, and showed the two glasses to the curious crowd. When I took a vote, 70 percent guessed the stream water correctly (I don't know how – maybe somebody peeked!). My point was well taken though, and when we said we had to leave, they begged us to answer more questions.

All in all, I felt confident that the nuns knew enough about water safety and personal hygiene to prevent illness under adequate living circumstances. So in this case, the problem stemmed not from ignorance, but from lack of resources and the poor conditions at the temporary dormitory. I hoped the diarrhea problem would abate once the new dormitory opened. In the meantime, we advised the nuns to use the filters and avoid drinking from the stream, no matter how crystal clear it looked. Most seemed to agree, and I felt satisfied that our visit was time well spent. As we headed back to the hospital, I thought about how best to push for more of these outings, which I found far more fulfilling than clinical work—not just because it got me out of the hospital environment once in a while, but because the focus was on prevention rather than cure. Lasting improvements in the health of the Tibetan community in exile would largely be through public health interventions, such as clean water and better housing, and I felt I needed to contribute to that effort in my small way.

4

Scarred

After my first several months in Dharamsala, I slowly began to realize that no matter how much Tibetan refugees tried to fit in to India, they were still outsiders in a huge subcontinent. I had met many fascinating elders, some who had fought against the Chinese occupation with CIA training in the 1960s and 1970s, or others who had fled across the Himalayas with their families only to face new challenges in their host country, India. One of them was Lhamo Tsering, an elderly man I saw several times as a patient. Apart from the Dalai Lama, he was the most remarkable Tibetan I met my entire year.[6]

Lhamo Tsering was a soft-spoken person, and was known for his gentle nature even while leading the Tibetan resistance movement in the 1960s. He became second-in-command to Gyalo Thondup, the Dalai Lama's older brother and the overall leader of the Resistance. His men, so I'm told, had tremendous respect for him. Lhamo Tsering was born in Amdo province in 1924. His village Nagatsang was close to Takster, the home village of the current Dalai Lama. Raised as a monk until the age of 8 in a predominately Chinese town, he spoke fluent Chinese and Tibetan. He studied at the Institute for Frontier Minorities in Nanjing, where he met Gyalo Thondup in 1945. In 1949, when the Communist forces closed in on Chinese major cities, he fled to Hong Kong through Shanghai. He narrowly escaped with the help of a harbor fisherman as Shanghai fell. He settled in Kalimpong, an Indian border town and center of the wool

---

[6] A more complete account in English of Lhamo Tsering's life can be found in Jamyang Norbu's Shadow Tibet: Selected Writings 1989 to 2004. New Delhi, India: 2004, pp 203-213.

trade with Tibet. After seeing the occupation of Lhasa first hand in 1952, he formed the Tibetan Welfare Association to oppose the occupation and initiate underground resistance activity inside Tibet. In 1958, he was among a small group of Tibetans who were secretly trained by the CIA in intelligence in Colorado and Virginia. When he returned to India in 1959, he organized an intelligence office in Darjeeling to liaise between the CIA and various resistance operations that were being launched against the Chinese from India and Nepal. This included intelligence gathering missions inside Tibet, and training resistance fighters in the remote kingdom of Mustang. Before the ailing Gompo Tashi Andrugtsang died in Darjeeling in 1964, he passed on the title of Commander-in-Chief of all Tibetan military forces to Lhamo Tsering. He expanded intelligence activities on the Indian and Nepalese borders with Tibet, set up a journal (*Gotok*) for the resistance movement called "Understand," and created a school for Tibetan resistance soldiers. When the CIA terminated support for the Tibetan Resistance in 1969 after President Nixon's visit to China, the resistance faltered but Lhamo Tsering pressed on. When the Chinese put pressure on Nepal to do something about the Tibetan guerrillas inside Nepal, Lhamo Tsering became the bargaining chip. He was arrested in 1974 as a hostage for the Tibetan guerrillas to disarm. He refused to coöperate, and sent messages to his forces to disregard his capture. When the Dalai Lama asked the guerrillas to give up their weapons, Lhamo Tsering was sent to prison in Nepal for 7 years for his role in the resistance. After his release in 1980, he moved to Dharamsala with his family and worked for the Tibetan Government-in-Exile in security matters, ultimately becoming the Minister of the Department of Security in 1993. Honest and conscientious to a fault, nearly every Tibetan I met regarded him in awe for what he had done. Although I did little more than adjust his blood pressure medication and give him a general check-up, it was a privilege to treat him.

I had also met some wonderfully gifted young people, cosmopolitan, well educated, and in many cases, trilingual (Tibetan, Hindi, and English). And I continued to meet incoming refugees, some so green and innocent that even their Tibetan countrymen considered them bumpkins. Granted, many Tibetans felt they were temporary inhabitants in India and had no obvious desire to assimilate into the Indian culture. Deep down, however, I think they all wanted to be accepted by their hosts.

Despite a very hospitable environment created by the Indian government, Tibetans had many political, legal, cultural, and financial hurdles to overcome, often on a daily basis. Assets were often left behind in Tibet. Entire families had to start over to build security for their children and elders. Education, both secular and religious, was often interrupted, and many refugees could not practice their previous occupations. For the young, life could be particularly difficult. Many youth were disaffected by the Tibetan political situation, feeling that the current Tibetan administration's policy toward engaging China over the future of Tibet would not lead to a satisfactory situation. They also felt disenfranchised from mainstream Indian society, born and growing up in India, but not really Indian. Importantly, a majority were frustrated by the lack of opportunities available to them for education and employment. Lastly, they still carried refugee identity cards, and were not able to obtain Indian passports. For a Tibetan, undertaking travel out of a country known for its mountains of paperwork could easily turn into a bureaucratic nightmare. I sympathized greatly with them because I was an outsider as well, although my situation in no way compared to the suffering that they were enduring.

There were other problems, too, in the "peaceful resting place" called Dharamsala. Somehow, I had assumed that Tibetans and Indians coexisted peacefully in this idyllic corner of the Indian Himalaya. On the contrary, some local Indian shopkeepers and politicians had been complaining for years that the region was becoming too crowded with the growing number of Tibetan refugees. The tension had reached its peak a few months before I arrived, when a Tibetan youth had stabbed an Indian in a dispute over a televised soccer game in which the "wrong" team won. The event was a spark for kindling that was ready to erupt in flames. In response to the stabbing, hundreds of local Indians rioted all the way up the hill from lower Dharamsala, destroying Tibetan property and looting Tibetan stores and buildings. Luckily no one else was hurt, but the event sent shock waves through both communities. The Dalai Lama went so far as to propose moving the entire Tibetan community to southern India, but this caused many businessmen and politicians to realize the importance of the Tibetan presence in bringing tourism and business to the area, not to mention international recognition. In a public ceremony, the Dalai Lama was presented with a petition asking him to stay. Ultimately there was a détente, with meetings between Indians and Tibetans that cooled the situation down. The Tibetan administration was compensated for the damage done during the riots, and agreed to temporarily suspend the admission of new refugees to the area.

The overt tension abated over the following months, but some of the underlying animosity remained. I discovered this first-hand one night on call, when two badly bruised Tibetan men drove up to the hospital. They stepped out of the car, and I sensed they had suffered injuries to both body and spirit.

"What happened?" I asked with concern, as they moved very slowly into my examining room.

"We were burying his dead baby near the river," the driver said, nodding toward the other man. "A group of young Indians attacked us. They stole a few thousand rupees and then..." The man looked at his friend, who was staring at the ground. "Then they dug up the baby's grave."

I stared at the pair in horror. To have a newborn die was bad enough. "How did you escape?" I asked.

"While they were busy digging and arguing with each other, we managed to run away. We think they wanted to kill us."

To make matters worse, I couldn't even treat the men's injuries if they wanted to file a police report. I was told that the Indian courts will only honor an Indian doctor's examination, not one done at a refugee hospital, let alone by a foreign doctor. Reluctantly I had to send them to the Indian regional Zonal Hospital down the hill.

When I told one of the Tibetan doctors in our hospital about the incident the next day, he responded that it was an "isolated event." This seemed like denial. As I at times discovered, some Tibetans seemed to prefer pretending that relations between themselves and their hosts were fine, rather than facing the need for a greater reconciliation effort between settlers and local Indians. Yet, it was obvious that strained relations were taking a toll on the Tibetan community. Six months after the riots, the McLeod Ganj Reception Center for new arrivals still had not reopened. At its peak, the center had processed and housed about 2,000 refugees a year, while they awaited placements in nearby settlements. Now the newest arrivals–many of whom had survived torture, abuse, and discrimination in Tibet, and fled across 19,000-foot Himalayan passes with little more than the shirts on their backs–were being held up at the Nepali border instead of being welcomed to Dharamsala with open arms. It was frustrating to think such an exhausting journey had to end in delay and further anxiety for those fleeing Tibet.

The Central Tibetan Administration (CTA) is the Government-in-Exile headed by the 14th Dalai Lama. The CTA has been based in McLeod Ganj, Dharamsala, since 1962, and claims jurisdiction over the entire Tibetan Autonomous Province and Qinghai Province, as well as parts of Gansu, Sichuan, and Yunan, all of which is termed "historic Tibet" by the CTA. The administration oversees schools, cultural activities, economic development, and health services, and provides welfare services for Tibetan refugees. The McLeod Ganj Reception Center is a central part of the services, receiving newly arrived refugees from Tibet and making arrangements for their care within India. The CTA is heavily dependent on financial aid from government and international institutions for its welfare work among the Tibetan exile community. The CTA is run by the Prime Minister's office, a position filled since 2000 through an election process. The CTA is composed of multiple ministries, such as Health, Education, and Foreign Affairs, with positions filled by appointment.

Eager for more information on the treatment of new arrivals, I made an appointment with Tsering Gyaltsen, the Secretary of the Department of Information and International Relations. He was featured in a well-known book about the Tibetan refugee experience written by John Avedon, *In Exile from the Land of Snows*. He had a welcoming air to him despite all the trouble he had seen. After exchanging formalities, we talked about the intake process for newcomers and the services (or lack thereof) for those who had been tortured. I asked him how I could put my medical skills to use for the good of the refugee community, and to benefit the human rights struggle of Tibetans in general. He felt I might be able to help record trauma stories for the Human Rights Desk, and introduced me to the department's director, Ngodup Palden. This office within the Government-in-Exile was charged with compiling human rights updates, writing urgent action alerts, and corresponding with other Offices of Tibet around the world regarding the human rights situation in Tibet. With this large scope of work, I expected to find a spacious office with several staffers. In fact, Ngodup Palden handled everything himself in one small office filled with stacks and stacks of paper and no filing space whatsoever. I couldn't imagine how he found anything, let alone distributed his urgent action alerts efficiently. Yet, he seemed well organized and promptly found his latest human rights update to show me.

"What I'm curious about is the process for new arrivals," I told him. "Does the Department of Security systematically talk to newcomers to get information about the current situation in Tibet, particularly regarding stories of imprisonment and torture?"

"Yes, there is a process," Ngodup Palden replied vaguely, "but the stories of torture don't get written down separately. You can find out more in the Documentation Center."

I pressed him on my real interest. "Is there any formal screening of refugees for signs of mental stress, such as depression or anxiety?"

"I can't say the process is formal. I think you should have a look in the Documentation Center." He directed me upstairs.

The Documentation Center was a surprisingly small room, considering that it was supposed to house all of the major human rights documents available concerning the Tibetan struggle for freedom. I found the filing system totally inadequate, with a staff not expeditiously responsive. Most likely they were terribly underfunded and the staff unappreciated, though I couldn't say why. They were reluctant to lend out materials, despite having several copies in some cases. I finally managed to convince the manager to let me take out one of their five copies of *Defying the Dragon*, the latest report by the Government-in-Exile on the condition of human rights in occupied

Tibet. I was eager to read it, as it was the most extensive report ever published by Tibetans on their view of the human rights conditions of their people. I still use the report as a reference, and feel that it gives me a clear picture of the abuses Tibetans have endured through the many years of Chinese rule.

Although it was well written, the Tibetans had a difficult time getting press coverage of the report in the West. The beginning of the pamphlet outlined the many years of suffering that the Tibetans had endured at the hands of the Chinese, including the years of starvation and forced labor in Tibet. It was an often told story but heartbreaking nonetheless. The core of the report was a description of the demonstrations that have occurred in Tibet since the late 1980s, when monks and nuns had a political awakening and began to directly challenge Chinese rule. A systematic pattern of arrests, abuse, imprisonment, and torture ensued, but it only made the resistance movement grow stronger. At the time of its publication, hundreds of political prisoners remained in Chinese prisons in dire circumstances, unable to safely practice their religion or culture. After some time, unfortunately, the information became outdated and was no longer "news" for the sound-bite oriented international media.

While I wanted to learn more, my daily clinical duties left me little time for further investigation. My call schedule was as rigorous as that of a medical intern in a busy U.S. urban public hospital. During my next call day (a 24-hour shift covering the emergency room and the hospital wards), I put casts on two children who had both fallen and broken a leg, treated a nun with diarrhea, educated a dehydrated Japanese tourist about oral rehydration salts, fit a donated ankle-stabilizing boot on a woman with a fracture, puzzled over a child with ankle edema of unknown origin, and admitted a young Indian woman who was severely malnourished for unclear reasons. Although my whole day and evening were spent on clinical care, I managed to get to sleep at a reasonable hour. As I drifted off from pure fatigue, I felt convinced that my real desire was to do more community health work, as well as a human rights research project that could be used for advocacy regarding torture survivors in the Tibetan refugee community. However, it was hard to deny the need to tend to the ill. I secretly hoped that with the end of the monsoon, people would stop getting sick!

No such luck. The following week, the hospital had three deaths in a single day, which made us all reevaluate the effectiveness of our own medical skills. Perhaps I had become overconfident in my medical abilities. One death was expected or at least not a surprise – a woman with drug-resistant tuberculosis. Patients with drug-resistant tuberculosis have fatality rates nearing 25 percent, so we were prepared for the worst. The next case, however, was a shocker. I had admitted a young boy for dehydration the night before. At 4:30 a.m. he got up and drank some water. About 2 hours later, Chokyi the nursing aide woke me to say the boy was complaining of abdominal pain. When I arrived in the ward a few minutes later, he was already dead but still warm. I stood stone-like, unable to comprehend what had happened. I ran to get help. Our resuscitation "crash cart" was woefully under stocked; we didn't even have adrenaline to help get his heart started again. The nurse and I stood there stunned, unsure of what to do next, or what to tell the family. It was futile to attempt anything drastic. To this day I can't figure out why he died.

The third death that day I only heard about. A 40-year-old woman had been given a test dose of penicillin by a nursing aide up the hill at the Tibetan Children's Village. Test doses are given to check whether the patient is allergic to a drug or not, and are usually made by pricking the skin with the drug. Unfortunately, she developed symptoms of anaphylaxis (hypersensitive allergic reaction, when an allergic rash is accompanied by a drastic drop in blood pressure and constriction of the airway), with a quick onset and severe shortness of breath. The Children's Hospital staff had rushed her into a hospital jeep and driven 20 minutes to Delek Hospital. By the time they arrived, her lungs had been squeezed shut by the allergic reaction. She was dead on arrival. I had given a talk earlier that week on how to treat anaphylaxis with a quick shot of adrenaline, making the tragedy all the more frustrating. It showed how unprepared the settlements were to deal with basic emergencies.

Thankfully, deaths were generally rare at Delek Hospital, and the following day proved to be much less harrowing. First, I diagnosed two cases of malaria. This was an unusual occurrence at 4,000 feet because the mosquitoes that transmit malaria to humans are generally unable to survive at such altitudes. One of the patients had amoebic dysentery as well – what bad luck to develop two tropical diseases at once, and not even in the tropics! Her double diagnosis violated the informal but often quoted rule in medicine called "Occam's Razor," which notes that the search should always be for a single unifying source of causation.

Later that session I saw a young German woman with nausea, diarrhea, and weight loss. She hadn't had her period in 2 months, was traveling with her boyfriend, but insisted they were not having sex. I suggested a pregnancy test anyway. When she never came back for the result, I figured I had made the diagnosis. I could hardly believe it when I heard the same story an hour later. This time, the woman was a recent arrival from Tibet who had been at Sogar School in the plains below. She claimed she had not had intercourse in the past 2 years. For her – dirt poor, with no education and no job prospects, and now pregnant – I truly felt sorry.

The real medical challenge came later in the day. A Nepali woman married to a Gurkha soldier arrived complaining of nose bleeds. She had had mitral valve surgery for rheumatic heart disease when they had lived in Hong Kong. For the past 4 years, she hadn't been on any type of cardiac treatment besides aspirin as a blood thinner. On exam, I detected a loud regurgitant murmur (from blood "regurgitating" backward through the valve into the main heart chamber) and a rapid heartbeat. I suggested that she go to Delhi for an echocardiogram to test the function of her mitral valve and the capacity of her heart. I was worried that lacking proper treatment, her condition might deteriorate rapidly, most likely leading to congestive heart failure. She followed our advice and promptly went to Delhi. I never received any follow-up from her either, and with the seriousness of her condition it was all the more important.

Meanwhile, a cross section of my inpatients could have been taken from any family practice textbook. In Room One we had Mingmar, whose X-ray indicated TB, then Karen, an Australian nurse with amoebic dysentery, and a second Mingmar (many Tibetans have the same name as there is a smaller list of names to chose from), whose main affliction appeared to be asthma. Room Two housed Jigme with malaria, Samdhup with alcohol-related ascites (fluid buildup in the abdomen), and Preeti, an Indian woman who believed she was ill, but whose real quandary was that her entire family had a drinking problem and left her with no money. In Room Three, Tenzin was still recovering from TB meningitis, while our paranoid monk, Tashi, continued to languish in the absence of any appropriate psychiatric facilities. Finally, our private room was occupied by a man with chest pain, who was waiting for his daughter to arrive from Switzerland and advise him whether to go to Delhi for a full cardiac work-up.

It was inevitable that a full patient load would coincide with a staffing shortage. I had witnessed this same phenomenon during my residency in Cambridge. Now that the cooler autumn weather had set in, we temporarily lost our chief lab technician and our pharmacist to the common Tibetan trade of selling sweaters. Every year Tibetans fanned out across the Indian subcontinent to sell sweaters in markets and roadside stalls during fall and winter. Ironically, the sweaters were made not by Tibetans, but by Indians in Punjab. It seemed even some of our hospital staff relied on the supplemental income to improve their economic situation. I did not blame them at all, but felt that some kind of staff backup should have been available.

Not long after the onset of the sweater-selling season, a man named Phuntsok came to the hospital with a spontaneous collapsed lung (pneumothorax). Treating this properly required inserting a chest tube between the ribs to remove the air from the space outside his lung, followed by several days of close observation while the lung expanded to its normal size. During this time, I developed a rapport with Phuntsok, and he eventually told me the story of his imprisonment in Tibet – something he had never shared with anyone before.

Four years earlier, Phuntsok had been arrested in Lhasa after his wool-exporting business began to do well. Why? The reason for his arrest was simple for the Chinese, but incomprehensible to those of us who believe in democracy and freedom of speech – he was found to possess a photo of the Dalai Lama. Phuntsok was held in a Chinese prison for 7 months and tortured nearly every day with beatings and an electric cattle prod. After his release he quickly escaped to India; he was now making a meager living as a tailor and keeping his past to himself. I decided to apply the Harvard Trauma Questionnaire, a mental health screening survey developed specifically for use in refugee populations that measures trauma experience and response, and calculates severity of post-traumatic stress disorder (PTSD) symptoms.[7]

The verbal questionnaire took us about 20 minutes to finish. It was somewhat simplistic, but I had no other way to determine whether he might have PTSD. After I added up his responses, the survey told me that he didn't have PTSD, though he scored high on the screening survey questions.

"Why haven't you told anyone about this before?" I asked. "When you first arrived, didn't the Security Department ask you whether you had been tortured by the Chinese?"

"They only asked one question about my trip over here. They didn't seem interested in details."

I felt frustrated that there was no effective system for collecting stories like Phuntsok's tale. It made me wonder whether the Government-in-Exile was doing enough to document Chinese abuses in Tibet. While the Security Department interviewed most new arrivals, very little information was passed on to the Human Rights Desk. Of equal concern, there was no mental health screening and psychiatric referral process for refugees who might need counseling. As I mentioned earlier, several nongovernmental agencies based in Europe were involved in the start-up of a Torture Victims Rehabilitation Project. But when I tried to learn more, the man in charge told me the

[7] The Harvard Trauma Questionnaire was devised in Boston for use with Southeast Asian refugees, but it has been adapted and validated for many regions. It inquires about a variety of trauma events, as well as the emotional symptoms considered to be uniquely associated with trauma. The questionnaire can be found at the website of the Harvard Program in Refugee Trauma.

program had enrolled just six refugees, and was providing medical care only, not counseling.

An exception to the poor documentation of survivor stories was the disturbing account of a young monk named Bagdro, who had given hundreds of interviews since his escape from Tibet in 1991.[8]

I first saw Bagdro when he met with a French television crew in a café overlooking the main temple (the Tsuglagkhang) of the Dalai Lama. He was nervous, visibly shaky. But it was his past, not the camera crew, that made him tremble.

I later had the chance to meet with Bagdro alone, when the lama of his dialectic school asked me to evaluate his mental status. Bagdro had been isolating himself, and some of his fellow monks were suggesting he turn in his robes. I talked with him for a long time in the privacy of his room at the monastery. He trembled constantly and kept his hands folded inside his robes to avoid notice. His voice was flat as he recounted his story for yet another well-meaning foreigner. His face only faintly reflected the pain he must have gone through.

Bagdro was born in 1968, the eldest son of a poor family living near the ancient Ganden Monastery. With Tibet under Chinese occupation, his parents had to beg for food, and one sister died of malnutrition. In 1986, Bagdro joined the Ganden Monastery, an enormous complex situated on a hillside near Lhasa. It once housed 4,000 monks, but had been decimated during the Chinese Cultural Revolution. Only 300 monks remained. Amidst these ruins Bagdro's religious and political education began. He engrossed himself in the study of ancient Tibetan texts, but it was a secret copy of the Dalai Lama's banned autobiography that moved him to work for the human rights of his people.

In the fall of 1987, following protests at other Tibetan monasteries, "political education" teams arrived at Ganden to quell any potential unrest. This crude brainwashing only solidified Bagdro's

---

[8] Details of Bagdro's life come from my personal interviews as well as from Ven. Bagdro's Hell on Earth: a brief biography of a Tibetan Political Prisoner, New Delhi, India: Indraprashta Press, 1998. His real name is used with permission.

commitment. During Lhasa's Great Prayer Festival in March 1988, Tibetan monks began spontaneous demonstrations against the continuing Chinese occupation of Tibet. Police dispersed the protestors with gunfire, and Bagdro, who was one of the protest organizers, was arrested.

During his first 11 days in detention, Bagdro was subjected to constant torture. An electric cattle prod was jammed into his throat while he stood on a wet floor. He was kicked all over his body. He was hung from his hands tied behind his back. He was forced to stand outside with his arms outstretched for 3 days. The police then kept him in handcuffs for a month, after which he went to trial and was sentenced to 3 years in prison. While in prison, he was beaten repeatedly, watched his compatriots take their last steps before being executed, and had his blood extracted against his will. His friends told him not to take part in prison demonstrations, but to escape and tell the world about Tibet. After his release in April 1991, Bagdro fled by foot across the Himalayas.

He arrived in India with TB and spent several months in the hospital regaining his strength. Frequent flashbacks and nightmares left him hyper-vigilant to stimuli, tremulous, and beset with concern for those he left behind. A visiting Western psychiatrist diagnosed PTSD, and well-intentioned foreign support groups raised money to send Bagdro to Paris for psychiatric care.

The encounter with cosmopolitan Europe changed Bagdro. He was prescribed several medications until his doctors found that the drug clomipramine appeared to help. His tale of torture and escape was disseminated, and soon he was giving interviews. He met heads of state and testified about his arrest and imprisonment before the Human Rights Commission of the British Parliament. It was difficult to tease apart the extent to which Bagdro was testifying out of his own desire to speak out about the human rights abuses suffered by Tibetans in China, or the desire of his sponsors to have a victim to trot out in front of the cameras. Perhaps some of the nongovernmental organizations needed a poster boy, and Bagdro served that purpose. For me, it was hard to imagine that being in a foreign country and having to repeatedly recount one's torture experience would be conducive to recovery from PTSD.

Nine months later, Bagdro returned to India better, but still ill. He ran out of medicine after several months and went into seclusion. After a year, fellow monks convinced him to take up his Buddhist studies again. But he was plagued by sudden episodes of fear, tension, and tremors. He was having trouble concentrating, which made his studies difficult, and he sometimes felt the need to isolate himself for weeks at a time.

Bagdro's illness contradicted the popular belief that Tibetan monks had an almost superhuman ability to withstand years of torture and yet survive psychologically. The monks' resilience was said to come from deep religious beliefs of compassion for all living beings, including one's enemy. Some Tibetan monks who were imprisoned after years of Buddhist training claimed the worst thing they experienced was nearly hating their torturers. One monk who survived two decades of imprisonment and torture told me, "Buddhism teaches you that your suffering is little compared with the suffering of others, and that the result of your suffering may even benefit others." This is a laudable state of mind; however, not one that all humans can hope to achieve.

Bagdro had completed very little Buddhist study at the time he was imprisoned. He told me he was completely unprepared to face the kind of torture he endured. Unlike more seasoned monks, he was psychologically unable to handle the strain. The result was a debilitating case of PTSD compounded by symptoms of generalized anxiety disorder. We agreed that he should go back on medication, though I felt what he needed most was counseling from a Tibetan-trained psychologist. As there were none that I knew of, I offered to meet with him regularly. He nodded and managed a smile.

Over the following weeks, Bagdro and I discussed the importance of continuing his religious studies and meditation. I pointed out that he was surrounded by hundreds of other monks in exile, many similarly traumatized, and they could help each other heal. Bagdro listened, but was sure a solution to his psychological problems must be European. He told me he was going to learn French, rather than Hindi.

Privately, I wondered whether Bagdro's time in France had been as helpful as he believed. While he had received excellent psychiatric care, the trip had also separated him from his culture, his community of fellow refugees, and his religious support structure – potential sources of strength during recovery from trauma. Perhaps his European supporters could have been of greater help by funding a local, culturally appropriate mental health program for Bagdro and his fellow torture survivors. After all, there were many other victims, and not every one of them could be sent to Europe for treatment. Now, at least, Bagdro would have the opportunity to benefit from Western medication while immersed in his own culture and his Buddhist studies.

After Bagdro had been back on antidepressants for one month, I saw him at the annual Uprising Day demonstration. What a surprise to see him actively involved! Soon he became one of the volunteers responsible for escorting ill monks to the hospital. He began to laugh again. His insomnia and anxiety lessened, and his concentration improved. When he held out his hand, the tremor was present but diminished. Eventually, he resumed giving interviews to visiting journalists and came to believe that telling his story might serve Tibet and bolster his will. His plight was a small inspiration to me, and kept me going with the belief that I might be making a small difference in the community, one person at a time.

5

Reaching the Community

By mid-fall, plague panic had engulfed Dharamsala, after an outbreak of the much feared disease caused by the *Yersinia pestis* bacteria occurred in the western port city of Mumbai (Bombay). Plague is an ancient affliction; there are reports of deaths from the dreaded disease on an epidemic scale as far back as the 6th century, when the plague of Justinian killed thousands as the Roman Empire began to disintegrate.[9]

In its most common form, plague causes black pustules and blisters to form all over the body (thus the term Black Death) before it turns inward and causes organ failure, septic shock, and death. It can also cause an infection of the lungs, called pneumonic plague, which is very contagious. This was the form being reported in Mumbai, with resultant panic across the city.

The "panic" in Dharamsala started despite the fact that there were no accounts of the outbreak reaching as far north as the Himalayan foothills. According to the papers, there had been 50 deaths in other parts of the country, and people were wearing masks in Delhi – cloth masks that probably kept out nothing but dust and dirt. I imagined the populace of our little community walking up and down the hillside in masks. It wouldn't have surprised me. We received so many daily requests for advice, especially from nervous Western tourists, that we almost felt the need to set up a separate plague clinic for the worried well. People everywhere tend to become highly worried about deadly diseases (Ebola virus, plague) that they have only a remote chance of catching, while remaining unconcerned

---

[9] For an excellent account of the effect of plague on the course of human history, see Hans Zinsser's *Rats, Lice, and History: A Chronicle of Pestilence and Plagues*; as well as Sheldon Watts' *Epidemics and History: Disease, Power, and Imperialism.*

about common conditions that are much more likely to cause harm such as the flu or auto accidents, for example.

As "plague fever" swept India, anyone arriving in our ER with a cough was labeled a "plague suspect" until the real culprit was diagnosed – usually flu, pneumonia, or TB. It didn't help matters when a young man from a nearby mountain village died of pulmonary failure within hours of arriving at our hospital. The paper called it Dharamsala's first plague death, even though it was ridiculous to assume he caught the plague in his isolated village. It was much more likely that the man had died of TB. Still, the panic button had been pressed, and our supply of tetracycline, the antibiotic used to treat plague, quickly dried up.

In a valiant attempt to restore calm in the local refugee community, the Tibetan Medical and Astrological Institute distributed thousands of "precious pills" meant to help Tibetans avoid the plague. These small balls of fermented herbs were wrapped with cloth and colored thread, and were meant to be worn around the neck. In a classic episode reflecting my ignorance of Tibetan medicine, I swallowed my pill one morning with my orange juice. It was extremely bitter, but the solidarity I felt with the locals was temporarily gratifying. I soon discovered, however, that I had made a mistake. My nursing aides were horrified when I told them that I had eaten mine. "But it was a pill, wasn't it?" I received a quick lesson about Tibetan herbal medicine pills after that. Some are meant to be worn in a pouch strung around one's neck, others to be consumed, and if you are unsure, it is best to ask first. Soon most of the Tibetan hospital staff and some of our Indian staff were sporting the multi-colored medicine balls. Perhaps they did work after all? Since we never had a plague case in Dharamsala, we will never know their true effect.

If Tibetans believed in the effectiveness of these herbal balls, I couldn't imagine why they didn't make some similar medicine for TB. In the Tibetan community, TB was a killer. The region's TB incidence (new cases per year) was about 65 times higher than in the U.S., and twice the rate of TB in India and China.[10]

---

[10] In the U.S., roughly one person out of every 20,000 people is diagnosed with TB each year. In Dharamsala, the figure is one out of every 300, an extremely high rate for a disease that is treatable and curable in over 95% of cases.

Discovering a new case of TB in Dharamsala was about as common as diagnosing diabetes in a typical U.S. internal medicine practice. The difficulty with TB, however, is that it can cause illness in many parts of the body and can mimic multiple disease conditions, leaving diagnosticians puzzled for weeks if not months. The medical literature is full of strange and uncommon presentations of illnesses caused by the *Mycobacterium tuberculosis* bacteria. During my first few months in India, I saw TB patients present to clinic with everything from a little bump on the neck, to conjunctivitis (inflammation of the lining of the eyeball and inner eyelid), to fistulas draining pus from abdominal abscesses, to pneumonia with a whole lung filled with fluid. It amazed me that something we scarcely thought about in the West was in this town the cause of so many deaths, so much pain, so much worry and dread.

While Delek Hospital had an excellent cure rate for TB (above 85 percent), there was no systematic testing of patients' close contacts (anyone who spent time near to the person, breathing the same air) and relatives as is standard practice in the U.S. Screening contacts for exposure to TB with a skin test can identify persons with TB infection early and permit treatment to prevent infection from progressing to disease. Screening persons with chest X-rays can identify subclinical disease early and allow for early treatment of TB disease before it worsens. There was a good argument for not doing screening, however. Because TB infection was so common, screening people who had come into contact with an infectious case could have resulted in testing large numbers of people with potentially little return. The public health literature on whether to test contacts of TB cases is still not conclusive. For the Tibetans, it was not cost-effective. Personally, as a physician, I was sure that more could be done to improve early diagnosis and containment of this disease that caused so many cases in the Tibetan community every year. I was therefore pleased when TB screening was the goal of my next field trip to a more remote Tibetan refugee settlement in the Indian Himalaya.

The destination was a settlement school with 500 students in Dalhousie. The drive took 6 hours on narrow, serpentine roads through Himachal Pradesh's craggy Dhalaudar Range. When we arrived, the sun cast an orange glow over the snowcapped Pir Panjal peak before dipping out of sight. We spent the night in the home of a rotund Tibetan welfare officer, who gave me my first chance to taste real *chang*. Our jovial host declined to drink with us, but shared several tales of his inebriated exploits as a young man. The cool air and tasty beer soon put me into a sound sleep.

The next morning, I began my assessment of TB among the schoolchildren. Despite the usual lack of a consistent potable water supply, the children looked fairly healthy. I only found cases of colds and upper respiratory tract infections, and the two staff nurses seemed competent to handle those on their own. That they were able to keep so many children generally healthy with such meager resources was impressive. The dispensary was stocked with a bare minimum of drugs, including just three types of antibiotics. They didn't even have enough money to buy vitamins or iron tablets for those with anemia. Fortunately, during 2 days of screening children with cough and fever, we did not find a single child with TB. This was good news, that an infectious case had not yet introduced TB into the school. It was possible, however, that our screening procedures were not adequate.

Back at Delek Hospital, if it wasn't one epidemic, it was another. In the few days that I was gone, dozens of people had shown up with conjunctivitis. The afflicted were of all ages: little kids, old folks, but mainly parents with children. The medical staff decided that the causative agent was most likely viral, as it did not respond to conventional antibiotic eye drops. With a limited medical cabinet to choose from, I resorted to prescribing steroid eye drops to ease the discomfort. While this was not exactly standard practice, it worked very well to calm the patients' fears and symptoms.

Our next epidemic of the week was mumps. I must have seen several dozen toddlers with swollen glands, many from the Tibetan Children's Village. Most of them should have had their measles-mumps-rubella vaccine series, the standard vaccine series given throughout the world. With so many cases of mumps, apparently they had not all been fully vaccinated despite the claims of the Health

Department. Now that they were sick with a virus, all I could offer was some reassurance and acetaminophen (Tylenol®, or paracetamol as it is known in India). Nowadays mumps is extremely uncommon in industrialized settings. In the U.S. there are typically less than 400 cases reported to the Centers for Disease Control and Prevention each year, or one case per 750,000 people. We were lucky that the cases were limited to mumps, as a measles outbreak occurring in such a limited space could have easily killed several children.

Meanwhile, back at Sogar School, we had to act fast to stem a malaria outbreak.[11]

Sogar School was considerably lower in elevation than Dharamsala, about 3,000 feet, where malaria mosquitoes were more plentiful. After we admitted three young men with very high fevers in succession, the hospital medical director decided to test every one of the school's 250 residents for malaria parasites in their blood (to detect any carriers). Though we found no new cases of malaria based on blood smears, we were limited by the quality of the laboratory equipment. In the end, to save time, we decided to put the whole school on prophylaxis. It was deemed more cost-effective to treat all the students, rather than test each one and treat only those who tested positive. Personally, I felt cleaning up the water supply would have been more important – Sogar School had far more cases of water-borne diseases like diarrhea and typhoid than malaria. This course of action, however, required many more resources and a great deal of effort.

A couple of weeks later, my colleagues and I could hardly believe it when diphtheria – a disease seen rarely if ever in the U.S. – appeared to surface at Sogar School. A Sogar student came to outpatient clinic with a sore throat, difficulty swallowing, a giant swollen neck, and fever. When the doctor on duty looked in the boy's throat, he couldn't believe his eyes. Encasing the entire throat was a pus-like membrane, adhered to the wall. I remembered being taught in school

---

[11] An outbreak is defined as an increase in the number of cases above the baseline. Because we usually only saw one case of malaria every other week, the occurrence of several cases in a row was enough cause for concern.

to look for that "pseudomembrane" (a false membrane in the throat) as a telltale sign of diphtheria. We sent the patient down to the Zonal Hospital for fear that he was about to suffer occlusion of his airway from the swollen "bull neck" that occurs in malignant diphtheria.

The next day, another student came in with a sore throat and inflammation. We had our new community health nurse take him to the Zonal Hospital for a throat swab. When the nurse returned, she reported that the first patient had been admitted to the general ward without isolation, and was only receiving erythromycin. The treatment of choice, diphtheria antitoxin, was available but hard to get – no point wasting it without first confirming the diagnosis. Since there were no culturing capabilities in Dharamsala, that meant waiting for the results of the throat swabs to come back from the adjacent mountain village of Shimla, 8 hours away by car.

In the meantime, I decided that the best public health course of action was to assess the situation at Sogar School with the help of the community health coordinator. If diphtheria was the cause of the infection in the first two students, it would be best to keep all the students confined at the school, which was isolated in the middle of farmland below the main Indian town. When we arrived, there were barely any students around. It was the second Saturday of the month and to Tibetans a holiday. Nearly all the students had left for McLeod Ganj. So much for containing an epidemic...

We talked to Lobsang, the school's health care worker, and took a tour of the area. We checked a few students in the dorms where the suspected cases lived, but found no one with sore throats or fevers. The place was nearly desolate, practically empty. If some of the students who had left for the weekend were carrying the disease, they were already spreading it to those they were in close contact with, and there wasn't much we could do about it. We discussed giving all the students antibiotics, but concluded that covering the whole school would just be too expensive. Until we knew more, we suggested Lobsang start only close contacts of the two suspected cases on low doses of erythromycin.

A few days ticked by without any new cases presenting. Just when we thought the erythromycin was working as prophylaxis against further possible diphtheria, a third person having a sore throat with a thick membrane came into our clinic. The young woman had a membrane covering her entire left tonsil. I volunteered to take her to the Zonal Hospital myself for a throat swab, so off we went. My plan was to try to commandeer some vaccine to take down to Sogar School for a mass vaccination.

In contrast to Delek Hospital, which was usually busy but organized, Zonal Hospital was mayhem. It was like taking a public hospital emergency room on a Monday morning, multiplying that by ten, and subtracting all the organization that is usually present in the West (i.e., procedures to sign in, sign consent forms, sit in the waiting room, get your blood pressure measured by the nurse, get seen by the provider, etc.). Pandemonium was the rule. Crowds of pushy men and women in saris jostled to get through one corridor to another. I found the ENT (Ear, Nose, Throat) clinic – actually just a room with a bench outside – and sat my potentially highly infectious patient down outside the door. I wasn't about to wait hours to get my case seen by a specialist, so I bulldozed my way past seven or eight people and sat down across from the ENT specialist's wobbly wooden desk. Once I introduced myself, the doctor took an interest and invited the patient in for an exam. I took my leave to go find some vaccine.

After instructions from five different people pointing me in seven different directions, I ended up going to the office of the Deputy Chief Medical Officer. He was a sturdily built man, but his nicotine habit gave him such a tremor that he seemed about to implode on himself. I told him who I was, and that I had just brought in a third possible case of diphtheria from Sogar School.

"I will not be surprised if we see more cases," I added, "unless we can start vaccinating these students."

His tremor worsened as he considered the possibilities. "If this really is diphtheria, I will have a giant headache on my hands in about a week." He called in several advisors, talked about going to Sogar to do throat swabs, and offered me as much vaccine as I wanted. Then he took a drag on his third cigarette in 15 minutes. "These Tibetans... they'll never leave. They have too much here."

It wasn't clear what he was implying. Too much what? Too much suffering as refugees in a huge country? Too much prejudice leveled against them for living in a strange land? Too much opportunity to catch diphtheria in a squalid refugee camp? I realized it was another case of an Indian who thought that the invited guests in his town were benefiting more from tourism and business than the locals. I didn't want to start a long discussion, so I managed to hold my tongue and went off to find my patient. After being examined by the ENT specialist, she had been sent to the lab. Now five doctors were hovering over this poor, newly arrived Tibetan refugee who could not utter a word of Hindi or English. All took turns shoving a depressor down her throat and taking a peek.

"Do you know of any other organism that forms that type of membrane?" I asked the group. I wasn't convinced it was diphtheria, but I couldn't think of any other possibilities.

One of the doctors claimed, "All these *new people* get this membrane when they get sick." I shook my head and took my leave. It wasn't the first time, nor the last, that I would encounter this outdated opinion that the Tibetans constituted a separate race of people. Having spent a mere 2 hours at the hospital, however, I felt we had made out like bandits with the vaccine in hand and a culture incubating in their laboratory.

The next morning, I headed to Sogar School with our community health nurse and a cooler full of diphtheria-tetanus vaccine. Lobsang was expecting us, and we quickly started forming the assembly line for students to receive their inoculation. Surprisingly, the newly arrived refugee students were terrified of needles. I had no idea why, nor could they explain their fear. This was in contrast to my experience at Delek Hospital, where patients (many of them long-time refugee residents of India) begged to have injections for their medical problems. In fact, Dharamsala was home to an immensely popular Indian doctor who basically practiced injection medicine. We had no idea what he gave people, but he offered injections to treat just about any condition – one shot per payment, of course. Our inner fear was that he was reusing needles in his practice, and thus potentially spreading viruses like hepatitis B or even HIV. For some reason,

Tibetans believed injections were the best medicine, the "strong medicine." Thus my surprise that the Sogar School students cringed and tried to run off when they saw the needles. Still, we managed to vaccinate about 170 students in 2 1/2 hours. Only one person fainted – a chronically ill man with cirrhosis from hepatitis B. As for the students who didn't show up, I hoped they would be protected by "herd immunity," the principle that you don't need to immunize 100 percent of a susceptible community against a disease in order to confer protection. Although diphtheria will strike any exposed person who is not immunized, our hope was that we vaccinated enough to prevent it from taking hold in this young and susceptible population.

About a month later, I confirmed our suspicions of diphtheria when I re-examined the woman I had taken to Zonal Hospital. She had developed swallowing and speech difficulties after her throat infection, textbook complications of diphtheria. At Delek Hospital we had no speech therapist, so there was little we could do for her. I gave her some encouragement, and told her that slowly over time her normal speech functioning would return. I often felt the only thing I could give my refugee patients was hope, so I tried to help her make the best of her situation. In the back of my mind, I knew that others had fared much worse, but I did not tell her that. With a smile and a handshake, she told me thanks for all I had done.

Throughout the odd assortment of outbreaks that dominated the fall, Delek Hospital continued to have staffing problems. When one of the other volunteer physicians found out his visa had expired and he was forced to leave; only two of us were left to handle all the work. At times, we found it nearly impossible to maintain order. One night, a newly admitted psychiatric patient locked herself in the delivery room and began throwing around precious equipment. Broken glass was everywhere. I was terrified we were about to witness a suicide, as we were unable to open the door from the outside. I finally convinced the patient to unlock the door and moved her to another room, where we provided her with a heavy dose of chlorpromazine to knock her out. I felt bad that I had to resort to chemical restraint for my patients in this small Tibetan community, but I felt that I had no other choice. Luckily, she calmed down that night, and we were able to get her on a regular schedule of anti-psychotic medications to control her symptoms.

At least I was off the next night and had the chance to go to a wedding. It was a Tibetan wedding, rather than a Western one, so in fact there was no one formal "ceremony." The entire weekend constituted the ceremony. The guests arrived at the first day's reception in the late afternoon and put thin white *kata* scarves on each member of the bride and groom's families for good luck. After several hours of "receiving," the wedding party ended up buried in about 100 scarves, quite an amusing sight. When all the guests had paid their respects, everyone sat down for food, *chang*, mahjong, and cards – I heard the Home Minister made a killing. Finally, the singing and dancing started around 9 p.m., once the feast was over, and all the single women had gone home.

A week later, I had almost as much fun when the opportunity arose to rescue a Mumbai (Bombay) math professor from a hypoglycemic seizure. I was headed to lunch one day, when 10 Indian men jumped out of a taxi van and carried their shaking, barely conscious friend into the hospital. The group presented me with a jumble of medicine bags (most pills in developing countries come in bags, not bottles, and they are usually not labeled) and an ID badge identifying the young man as having diabetes. Generally, mental status changes observed in a diabetic imply hypoglycemia (low blood sugar) until proven otherwise. I gave him an intravenous glucose infusion (dextrose-10%). Within 15 seconds, he was talking to me as if nothing had happened. This simple yet extraordinary method of pulling someone out of a hypoglycemic stupor is one of the most satisfying interventions one can do in the practice of medicine. Just give a little sugar, and the patient is instantly revived. It turned out the 23-year-old professor was in Dharamsala on holiday, and he was eager to jump up and dash off with his friends. I was afraid that might be a setup for a repeat, so I told him I'd let him go only if he ate lunch and waited 2 hours. He refused any more intravenous glucose. After all our arguing, he invited me to lunch. We shared some *chapatis,* and he was off.

Despite the staffing shortage at the hospital, I managed to continue my visits to the outpatient clinic in McLeod Ganj. Because the area was popular with tourists as well as Tibetan settlers, the clientele was varied and often very colorful. One afternoon I met a Ugandan who claimed to be "the Private Secretary of His Imperishable Gloriness, Bambi Baaba, founder of Spiritual City, Uganda, the Saint of Africa." I didn't argue with him – he might have convinced himself that this is true, and for all I knew it might be. However, I was in no mood to quarrel or get into a convoluted discussion about sainthood or how to be canonized. I wanted to focus on his medical problems. After touring India for 7 months, the man said he was sick of the food, feeling tired, and not sure what to do. He was a vegetarian and looked awfully pale, which is more difficult to detect in an African with darker skin tone. A blood test confirmed severe anemia, and when he confessed to a craving for beans, I told him that would be just the thing. Since beans were not frequently on the menu at any of the local eateries, I suggested he buy some at the market and cook them himself. This private secretary (of an imperishable gloriness) looked at me strangely, thought for a second, and then agreed he could find someone in his entourage to help him. I prescribed him some iron and sent him happily on his way.

Not all of my consultations ended so amiably. When a young mother came in with the worst breast infection I had ever seen, we got into a heated argument over her delay in seeking medical care. Not only was she sick, but she was feeding her newborn from the same breast. He had developed a large abscess on his right cheek, with pus leaking all over his face. I told her I wanted to admit her and the infant for intravenous antibiotics, but she refused, saying she had two other children to take care of at home. I pleaded for the baby's sake, and she finally agreed to go down to Delek Hospital. I later found out that she showed up without the baby, was given ampicillin, and left. I could only hope the baby's abscess was going to drain on its own. Without follow-up on our patients we were left wondering if the treatment we prescribed actually worked, and if the patient recovered. I was particularly worried about the woman's child, but I could not find anyone at Delek who knew who she was or where to find her.

After work that day, I made a house call to the owner of a giant hotel in McLeod Ganj. He even sent a car to fetch me, despite the short distance from the hospital. I didn't want to become known among local Tibetans as catering to the Indian elite, so I hid behind the tinted windows of the car that drove me the 3 minutes to the hotel. The owner's suite was spacious, filled with ostentatious Indian décor. I had the feeling that the whole place would be covered in mildew if it were not cleaned daily. The owner was a man of about 45 years. He mixed his life story in with his medical history so intricately that it didn't take long for me to tire of Coke, cookies, and ennui. To be fair, he had a real concern: his father had died of heart failure at the age of 55. Luckily, he had no other risk factors except a moderately elevated cholesterol level. His real problem appeared to be stress. He admitted that running a giant hotel was often nerve-wracking, with so much money on the line, and he sometimes took diazepam (Valium®) to help him sleep. My intervention turned out to be mostly preventive in nature, a good relief from prescribing antibiotics all day to ill refugees and tourists. I made sure he wasn't smoking, and recommended he start a mild exercise program to keep his cardiovascular system in shape. The harder part was convincing him that slimming down would be helpful. In India, being overweight is a sign of financial success and riches. The concept of maintaining a lean figure for your health was only beginning to catch on in the Indian subcontinent, and only slowly. In India (as in China), to be corpulent is a sign of wealth.

The following week, I used my day off to attend the Dalai Lama's teaching to a group of monks visiting from France. The entrance requirements were steep. One had to have had formal Buddhist training or a great deal of meditation experience, neither of which I had. There were many visitors that did meet those requirements, as Buddhism is now a fast growing religion in the West. Much of the attraction to study came from the charisma and message of peace of the Dalai Lama himself, but others were becoming followers due to what they perceived as the lack of spiritual values of Western commodity-centric materialism. Buddhism teaches selflessness, compassion, and service. Many start their new spiritual journey in Dharamsala. No one had a precise figure as to the number, but hundreds of Westerners came to study Buddhism at the Dialectic School or the Tibetan Library every year. Their presence made our village somewhat a place of pilgrimage for new and old initiates alike.

Being a novice, I decided to try to pull some strings to be admitted. I remembered that one of my professors back in Cambridge had treated the brother of the head of security for TB. I mentioned this to the head of security at the entrance gate and was let in easily.

The teaching, which had been taking place all week, was on Je Tsongkhapa's Great Treatise on the Stages of the Path to Enlightenment or *Lamrim Chenmo*, a foundational text on how to meditate and include daily religious practice in your life. A simultaneous English translation was provided by His Holiness' official translator Lakhdor, and broadcast via a low-power FM radio transmitter to listeners within a 100-yard radius. The day I attended, the teaching focused on patience, accepting faults in others, concentration, cleansing the mind, and some specifics of higher Tantric practice. The day was divided into a 3-hour morning session that began with chanting, then a longer afternoon teaching, during which time many became somewhat somnolent. My first impression, besides the beauty of the temple teaching room and the splendor of His Holiness' throne, was that the French Buddhists' chanting couldn't hold a candle to the Tibetan monks.

Buddhism is not native to Tibet (or to France for that matter!). The earliest recorded influence of Buddhism in Tibet was during the rule of Songtsän Gampo (617-649 A.D.), who married the Chinese princess Wen Cheng and founded the first Buddhist temples in the region. His successors were equally enthusiastic about Buddhist influence, and thus Emperor Trisong Detsen (755-797 A.D.) established Buddhism as the official religion of the state. Tibetan Buddhism evolved into four main traditions, the Nyingmapa (the oldest and original order), Kagyupa, Sakyapa, and Gelugpa. The Gelugpa order of Mahayana Buddhism was founded by Je Tsongkhapa as a reform movement within Tibetan Buddhism and emphasizes strict monastic discipline and the notion of an ever-present bodhisattva[12]

---

[12] A bodhisattva is a being that compassionately refrains from entering nirvana in order to guide others and is worshipped as a deity in Mahayana Buddhism.

guiding sentient beings toward enlightenment. The Dalai Lama is from the Gelugpa order. Those interested in learning more are best counseled to read a scholarly text on the subject, as it is not my specialty! The Dalai Lama is the temporal and spiritual leader of six million Tibetans (and Buddhist non-Tibetans). It is commonly accepted that the title "Dalai Lama" was bestowed by the Mongolian ruler Altan Khan upon Sonam Gyatso, the 3rd Dalai Lama, in 1578. Each successive Dalai Lama was believed to be the reincarnation of the former, forming a long line of Buddhist masters who have become so enlightened as to be exempt from the wheel of life and death. The succession has continued to the present day.

In contrast to the Western Buddhists and their subpar chanting, the Dalai Lama lived up to my expectations. His teachings were clear and easy to understand, even for a beginner like me. I felt fortunate for the chance to see him in his supreme role as a leader of the Mahayana Buddhist Gelugpa order. I silently hoped to arrange a private meeting before my stay in "Little Lhasa" was over. His aura was remarkable, his laugh staid but giddy at the same time, his smile impenetrable. I couldn't help but have a small bounce in my step after being in the same room with him for 8 hours.

The bounce didn't last long, however. The next few weeks brought me back to reality, as they were filled with challenging medical cases. One of the saddest was a newborn whose young parents brought her to Delek Hospital with a broken leg. They had no idea how it had happened. Because of the delicate nature of the break, we sent her down to Zonal Hospital for casting, where they did a very good job. But the baby was back 2 days later with three new fractures – in the opposite leg's femur, tibia, and fibula. We couldn't believe our eyes, and the parents seemed just as bewildered. After some deliberation among the staff, we realized we were dealing with a case of osteogenesis imperfecta, a congenital "weak bone" disease (also known as "big bone disease" due to the bone overgrowth that occurs to make up for the weakness) not uncommon in Tibetans. In severe cases, bones can break inexplicably during the course of an ordinary day. We sent the family to the nearest university medical center for a full workup. The baby would have to remain in a cast for at least the next 6 months, and probably faced a difficult and painful future. I could think of nothing else to do for that family. I was heart-broken. Seeing young children sick and in pain is one of the hardest moments in medical practice for me.

During a chaotic call day, I was soon forced to face one of my worst fears... again. A young Indian woman arrived in labor, and – you guessed it – the power went out. As if Murphy's Law were the law of the land, she was ready to push just as the sun went down. So out came the flashlights. The poor patient must have been terrified lying in our cluttered delivery room with beams of light fluttering around her through the darkness. This was her first baby and she had no attendants other than her grandmother, who in the end was no help at all. I let the nurses do most of the coaching, and when it became apparent that we needed to do an episiotomy I bit the bullet and cut open a wider vaginal opening to facilitate the delivery. I can't think of a more painful minor procedure, for the patient as well as the doctor. In this case, however, it was completely called for.

The baby came out with the umbilical cord wrapped around its neck. I quickly cut the cord, and the umbilical blood sprayed up into the air and onto my glasses. The baby was fine and the mother relieved to be finished with the delivery. But she was ultimately disappointed when the gender became known. A girl. It bothered me so much to see her groan – not the reaction one hoped to get from the new mother of a healthy baby. Once the afterbirth was out, I had to sew up the perineum by the light of a single beam. If only my obstetrical professors in medical school could see this!

As if the birth by flashlight weren't excitement enough, there were three more deliveries the following week. First, a young Tibetan woman came in 12 hours after her membranes ruptured. She progressed slowly, and we decided to speed things up so her labor wouldn't go on for more than a day. Susan, one of the other volunteer physicians, hung a bag of oxytocin (to induce contractions of the uterus) and left the patient alone with a nurse. The mother finished her first stage of labor in a few minutes, passed through the second stage in less than half an hour, and before anybody noticed, had her baby right in her undergarments! Susan walked in when she heard a cry. She pulled up the woman's *chuba*, and there was the baby, soaked in blood but breathing well and looking as if everything was going according to plan.

Next, a young Indian woman came to the hospital after having labor pains for 16 hours. Michael, our new doctor from England, ushered her into the delivery room, and while he was out getting ready to do an examination, he heard shouts. He rushed into the room, and the baby's head and one arm were already out, with the baby wailing away like mad. He deftly handled the rest of the birthing process, and in the end was quite proud of his first Tibetan delivery.

Then it was my turn again, and at least I was in the room when the baby appeared. We joked that it was the first doctor-attended birth all week. The mother was a young Indian, and the baby was another girl. Since I always seemed to deliver girls, I realized that I might be getting a reputation in the local community for delivering girls to disappointed parents. I could never open up an obstetrics practice in India – no one would come.

The following Friday, a young Tibetan woman came to our antenatal clinic for the first time. While I was trying to calculate her delivery date, one of the nurses pointed out that the patient was the bride at the wedding I had attended last month. I hadn't recognized her because she had been covered in hundreds of white *kata* scarves at the ceremony. Those scarves had scrupulously concealed her belly as well as her face. She must have been about 5 months pregnant at the time, and I was probably the only one in the room who didn't know it. Although Dharamsala was a refugee community, news traveled as fast as in any other small town.

Many of the nurses had tried to convince me that the local young women didn't have premarital sex, but what more evidence did I need? The problem was that if an unmarried woman wanted birth control, she had to request it from our head nurse, which was equivalent to placing a full-page ad in the local newspaper. The result was that more than a few young women ended up taking their chances with the "natural method" of birth control.

By the time the mornings started to have a chill in the air, we were still terribly short-staffed despite the arrival of two new volunteer physicians to Delek Hospital. I was needed at the hospital and clinics day and night, making it nearly impossible for me to continue meeting with the Human Rights Desk or offering health education to new arrivals. I felt my research into the human rights abuses suffered by Tibetans, and opportunities to improve public health on a more community-wide scale, were effectively cut off due to the long hospital work hours. My human rights fellowship was turning into a purely clinical experience, and I slowly began to lose interest in the work. Outpatient clinic was particularly tedious. Some days I saw 60 patients with the same problems: colds, TB, anemia, or diarrhea. Prescribing metronidazole antibiotic for dysentery and dicloxacillin antibiotic for skin infections made me feel more like a machine than a doctor with a recent master's degree in public health. I believed in primary care medical practice, but I didn't think that it was going to solve all the Tibetans' health problems. I felt stuck in a never-ending merry-go-round of patching people up only to send them back to the conditions that made them ill in the first place. I didn't want to get stuck in biomedicine.

The dominant paradigm of biomedicine is based on a reductionist definition of health that emphasizes the central role of health services. Health is defined solely as the absence of disabling disease or death. This is insufficient, in that it does not include the social and economic context of ill health, and does not acknowledge the health consequences of poverty. Conversely, the World Health Organizations' definition of health is more holistic, and states that "Health is a state of complete physical, mental, and social well-being and not merely the absence of disease or infirmity." Furthermore, the 1978 Declaration of Alma-Ata states that, "Health...is a fundamental human right and that the attainment of the highest possible level of health is a most important world-wide social goal whose realization requires the action of many other social and economic sectors in addition to the health sector." What the Tibetans truly needed to improve their health situation was to have their rights respected. I tried to carry the spirit of this declaration with me every day I was in Dharamsala.

Just as I began to question whether my medical efforts were worthwhile, a chance meeting renewed my enthusiasm and boosted my spirits to face the cold winter ahead. I had been walking briskly up the *lingkor* path on my way to McLeod Ganj, when I started to pass two slow-moving monks. I turned to look at them, and to my surprise, one was Tenzin, the monk who had until recently been laid up at Delek with TB meningitis.

"Wow," I exclaimed, "you're walking!"

Tenzin responded with a smile that conveyed both gratitude and happiness. I took his arm to help him up the steepest part of the path, and we had a conversation in broken Tibetan. Not only were his fellow monks taking him for his daily streptomycin shots, they were actually following my suggestions regarding physical therapy. To see that he was trying so hard to get better, that he had found the strength to walk again, made my day – no, my whole month. I felt a renewed sense of purpose. I realized that even if I never got the chance to leave behind something larger than a few band-aids, healthy newborns, and healed bone fractures, I was touching the lives of those I cared for – and they were touching mine.

6

Small Victories and Setbacks

By any stretch of the imagination, it was an extraordinary meeting for me. I had repeatedly asked the private secretary for an audience with His Holiness, the fourteenth Dalai Lama of Tibet, but had been turned down due to his busy schedule. I had heard rumors that it was easier to get an audience with the Dalai Lama than with, for instance, Nelson Mandela, who wouldn't see just anyone wishing to talk about the politics of national liberation. The Dalai Lama, I had heard, was willing to talk dharma with nearly anyone who wanted to do so. He kept an extremely busy visitation and lecture schedule. My request for half an hour of his time, however, came in the middle of a busy fall schedule for the living Buddha, one in which he traversed several continents in a matter of months. The office of security finally granted our request only when the winter had settled in. My American colleague here to work with the Tibetan Women's Association, Elizabeth Fabel, and I were happy just to be able to see him.

The security check at the front gate was rigorous and somewhat surprising, considering that I had been working in Dharamsala since the summer and was well known in town by several governmental-in-exile officials and many Tibetans. I forgot all of that when I was allowed into the inner sanctum. The grandeur of the Dalai Lama's domicile became apparent as soon as I entered the waiting area outside the reception hall. The large *thangka* paintings on the wall were stunning, the room spotless, and the flowers outside the window seemed particularly fragrant. Newsletters by Tibet support groups from around the world lay in a meticulous fashion on the coffee tables, as if no one had bothered to open up the pages to read the contents. Several German journalists were trying to have a conversation with a young assistant secretary, who had an air of self-importance that seemed inappropriate for such a spiritual place.

After a short wait, it was our turn to walk out on the porch that led to the Dalai Lama's sitting room. As I approached, I saw him peeking around the doorway with his effervescent smile. He was a little chubbier and shorter than I had imagined, and his socks were bunched up toward his shoes, but he was radiant. He extended his arm – what a pleasure to shake hands with a recipient of the Nobel Peace Prize!

"*Tashi delek.*"

"*Tashi delek!*" I said delightedly.

His hands were soft, his grip gentle but firm. I couldn't help but stare at the fantastically beautiful receiving room, with all the splendor one can imagine the leader of Tibet might have in his house. He invited me to sit on the long sofa, next to his single cushioned chair, with his translator sitting opposite. It was difficult to focus solely on His Holiness when I found myself surrounded by all the trappings of one of the world's great spiritual leaders. Once we were sitting, I tried to concentrate exclusively on my discussion with him. I couldn't help but notice, however, that His Holiness seemed to have the body language of someone with indigestion, complete with that glazed over look in his eyes. I don't mean to be irreverent, but the moment captured for me a feeling that despite being the living Buddha and holy protector of Tibet, here was a regular human male dealing with a bad lunch.

He looked rather tired, having just returned from England, where he told an audience that he would step down as Tibet's political leader if needed. His path of nonviolence had not brought the Tibetans any closer to returning to their homeland, and some within the exile community, especially the young and unemployed, were calling for armed rebellion against the Chinese. I had spoken with some of these revolutionaries during my time in Dharamsala. I was considering whether or not I could bring up this subject, when the Dalai Lama let out a large yawn, then looked at me with his playful smile. I decided not to talk politics, even though that is what I really wanted to do. Instead we spoke about where I had come from, my decision to volunteer in the Tibetan refugee hospital, and the type of work I was doing there. He responded in Tibetan, using his secretary as a translator, which surprised me because I knew his English was good. I began describing some of my patients and decided to tell him about the number of Tibetans I had seen with depression.

"Many of them turn out to be torture survivors," I explained. "I'm concerned that Dharamsala has no mental health services for these patients."

It was difficult for me to tell what he thought about this observation, for initially he made no reaction. Tibetans expect monks and lamas to serve as counselors when necessary, and you couldn't have found more monks in one city if you tried. I imagined that His Holiness probably expected the monks in his monasteries to take care of their own. I decided to take a different approach.

"Do you have any suggestions on how I can treat these survivors of violence when I come across them? I only know how to evaluate them for depression and anxiety disorders from our Western point of view. Are there symptoms of mental distress particular to Tibetans that I should look for?"

"Let me think," he replied. He shared his concern that monks and nuns who had been tortured did not have good concentration in their meditation practices and religious studies. He spoke for a few minutes about *samsara* or suffering, which Tibetans consider to be an inherent part of life. I couldn't ascertain whether he felt that encountering violence was a fact of life. I wanted to explore the point more fully, but our time together had quickly elapsed.

After a few quick photo snaps, I was rushed out by the secretary, feeling disappointed that the meeting had gone by so fast. There was so much more I wanted to discuss. I reminded myself that a private conversation with the Dalai Lama was a once-in-a-lifetime experience, and I was lucky to have had the opportunity at all. I felt like I was on a high for several weeks after.

A couple of weeks before the long-awaited meeting, I had taken advantage of beautiful weather and 2 full days off from the hospital to trek up to Indrahara Pass, high above McLeod Ganj. I asked two companions to join me, an Indian guide and a Frenchman named Jean-Claude. The first afternoon I was ready to stop when we reached 9,000 feet, but our guide wanted to press on. My pack was weighing me down, and I didn't know how much further I could hike. At 11,000 feet the altitude suddenly hit me like a thick cloud. The air was clear, but I was winded and exhausted. I just plodded along at half my usual pace, hoping that the slope would level out or at least produce a shady tree to lean on for a few minutes. By late afternoon we hit a plateau, and the Dhauladhar Range loomed ahead of us. We pitched camp during the twilight hour, as the waxing moon rose toward Venus. Our guide cooked a hurried curry without any turmeric, and we went to bed much too early. I was giddy with exhaustion, but the decreased oxygen concentration at that altitude made it tough to fall asleep.

For some odd reason, while I was surrounded by the clear air of the Himalaya, my thoughts drifted to Delhi, a city with the thickest smog I'd ever seen. The sun never seemed to shine directly on Delhi. It just glowed through a thick orange haze. I remembered the air being so dirty it had discolored my clothing, face, nails, and mucus membranes. There, it had been the pollution that strained my lungs and clouded my mind. Here, it was the thin air. But at least this air was clean. It was hard to believe such purity existed in the same country that hosted refugee "towns" like the Majnukatilla neighborhood in Delhi, where several thousand Tibetan squatters made their homes on the banks of the rancid Yamuna River. I had spent a couple of hours roaming the settlement during a weekend visit to Delhi. I vividly remembered the large families living in tents that were practically on top of each other. Women had been crouched around open fires heating tea, while naked children shat green slime into the drain gullies. The men, mostly unable to find jobs, began the day drinking *chang* in bars that blared Indian Bollywood music. The clean, quiet plateau seemed light years away.

At around 9 p.m., my thoughts were interrupted by a low growl outside. "A leopard," our guide said calmly. This did little to cure my insomnia.

The trek became more tough on day two. There were no more trees, just snow and ravens. The goal, Indrahara Pass, stood at an elevation of 15,120 feet straight up the side of the mountain. We started early in hopes of avoiding the clouds that tended to obscure the view by mid-morning. I soon became winded, as did Jean-Claude, though his French Pyrenean blood made him better prepared for the altitude. Despite his fatigue, he seemed to bound up the hillside like a mountain goat. My pulse and respiratory rate kept going up, now matter how slowly I walked. I couldn't help but imagine what would have happened if I walked into an ER in that state. "Quickly! His pulse is 150 beats per minute, his blood pressure 110, respiratory rate 40 breaths per minute, he must be in atrial fibrillation, no, pulmonary edema, no, oh man! For 3 hours, you say? My god, it's a pulmonary embolism!" That would have been the likely response of any ER resident physician. I wouldn't have made it out without a barrage of tests, but here on the mountain, it was just the three of us and the slope and the clear indigo sky.

It felt better to keep going than to stop. There was something intoxicating about the rhythm of going up a 45-degree slope, thin air aside. I could hardly believe it when, after just 2 1/2 hours, we reached the pass. The view of the Pir Panjal range to the north in the early morning sun was stunning. Mount Kinor Kailash, at 18,550 feet in the foreground, lived up to its designation as the holy, unclimbable Shiva mountain. Behind us, the rest of India spread out like a green carpet to the misty horizon. We sat down and meditated on the scene. I couldn't believe we had climbed 9,000 feet in less than 24 hours. It was a humble and inconsequential feat compared to what others have accomplished in the Himalaya, but personally satisfying nonetheless.

I slept much better that night, having acclimatized somewhat to the altitude. I was still a bit lightheaded, which was to be expected, but luckily I didn't have a headache. Dinner was rice with *dal* (lentils) and vegetables. We had so much left over, we were able to share with the construction workers we met who were building a trekking hut nearby. I slept soundly. The next morning the frost on our tent didn't melt until 8 a.m., when the sun finally made it over the mountains to shine on our campground. The walk down exacerbated my old knee injury, so I couldn't go down more than 1,000 feet per hour. We made it back to Dharamsala in the early evening, and I had dinner with Jean-Claude before returning to the hospital.

As it turned out, my mountaineering partner was involved with a Planète Enfants project to improve the community health workers' water-borne disease management skills. Jean-Claude's expertise was in water management and testing, and he asked me for the names of doctors who would be willing to talk about the diagnosis and treatment of water-borne diseases. I volunteered immediately, sensing the type of public health opportunity I had been looking for all along. I went home and drew up a plan for a teaching schedule and role-playing games to get the health workers involved with learning, instead of having them just sit around listening to didactic lectures.

A week later, just days before my highly anticipated meeting with the Dalai Lama, I developed a mysterious fever and chills that sent me to see a Tibetan doctor for the first time. I assumed it was a virus, which no allopathic practitioner could treat, so for the experience I though I would try a Tibetan medical doctor. I made an appointment at the Tibetan Medicine and Astrological Institute with Dr. Tsewang, the daughter of a famous doctor of Tibetan medicine. Her waiting room was full of jars of red and brown herbal balls in an array of pill-shaped sizes. She ushered me in after a short wait. I immediately liked her delicate manner. She offered me tea, not realizing that I had come for a consultation instead of a chat about one of our common patients. I rubbed the tender, apricot-sized lymph node on the left side of my neck.

"I can't figure out what I've got," I told her. "It's like I have the flu with a vengeance – body aches, a runny nose, congestion, sinus pain, and alternate periods of shaking and sweating puddles. My fever has been up to 102 degrees Fahrenheit."

"How long have you had the congestion?" she asked.

I got slightly annoyed that she was ignoring my fever. "Almost 2 days, but the fever has been present the entire time as well."

"Let's take a look."

Dr. Tsewang took my pulse for about one minute, as is the tradition, then quickly proclaimed that I didn't need any medicine. I knew she was probably right, but it's not what I wanted to hear.

"Isn't there anything I can try?" I asked, in the hopes that Tibetan medicine might have something to ease my symptoms. I left with my expectations dashed.

For a second opinion, I sought out Dr. Kunga Gyerme, a physician recently arrived from Tibet who had opened a private practice in McLeod Ganj. In his 50s, he seemed a master compared to the young Dr. Tsewang. He asked four or five questions about sleep patterns, constipation, and body pain. Then he held my arm on the desk and gently placed three fingers over my wrist's radial artery as if he was playing a cello. I closed my eyes. I could feel him varying the pressure with each finger, judging the quality and character of the three main energy (*chi*) meridians on each arm. I felt I was in the hands of a virtuoso. His diagnosis in the end: *rLung*, loosely translated into English by some as "affliction of one's air, or stress." I became disappointed again, but it was mainly out of ignorance.

In traditional Tibetan medical practice, *rLung* is commonly described as a subtle flow of energy, mostly connected with air. However, it is not simply the air that we breath or the wind in our stomachs; it goes much deeper than that. *rLung* is like a horse, and the mind is the rider. If there is something wrong with the horse, then the rider will not be able to ride properly. The general function of *rLung* is to help growth, movement of the body and exhalation and inhalation, and to aid the function of mind, speech, and body. *rLung* helps to separate in our stomach what we eat into nutrients and waste products, and it regulates that balance in the body. The nature of *rLung* is both hot and cold. It is rough, light, cool, thin, hard, and movable. The theory, however, was beyond my understanding at that moment. I felt sick in the present, but the physician was looking at my broader state of health.

"But I've been having fevers," I pointed out. He didn't waver in his diagnosis. For a Tibetan physician, the truth was in the pulse that he had meticulously taken. I left with medicine in both pockets, yet little hope of relief. My fevers continued on and off for several days, then miraculously disappeared just in time for my face-to-face with the Dalai Lama. Perhaps both doctors were right about there being nothing inherently "wrong" with me besides stress. We now know that there are intricate connections between the psychological, neurological, and immunologic systems. I was likely feeling a bit of elevated stress from working and living outside my home country for an extended time period. That stress could have easily manifested itself with various somatic (physical) symptoms.

On my first day back on call there were fortunately no new admissions, just a full day of school entrance physicals for newly arrived Tibetan teenagers. I gave each of them some pointers on staying healthy, knowing it was likely the only health education they ever received. I also had a rare conversation with a sexually active Tibetan girl, who came in complaining of vaginal discharge. It turned out she and her partner were using no birth control at all. She was totally at risk, and not just for pregnancy. I couldn't get the girl to agree to any kind of exam, but at least we talked.

A few days later, I got word that Jean-Claude's water-borne disease training was going forward. I was concerned that the Tibetans had not had a chance to contribute to the course design, but the Department of Health didn't seem to mind and had already made arrangements to bring in health workers from Tibetan communities around India. I was also concerned that I might have trouble getting time off from the hospital to participate, but I was able to wiggle a few days free during the second half of the 2-week course. Jean-Claude spent the first week talking about the design of water filtration systems, how to construct a well, how to purify water, etc. The health workers seemed to enjoy it, especially the field trips to nearby camps. A doctor from the Department of Health then spoke about constructing latrines. Finally, it was my turn to discuss the various kinds of diarrheal illnesses one can contract from unclean water. Noninflammatory diarrhea and cholera are characterized by profuse watery diarrhea and pain, the latter much more so than the former. Diarrhea accompanied by blood could be any number of things such as inflammatory diarrhea, bacillary dysentery, amoebic dysentery, or typhoid. It took a fairly experienced clinician to discern the difference.

The nine health workers in my first class were all women. They struck me as young, not fully mature, and not comfortable expressing their own opinions. As is the custom, they sat dutifully and silently in class, too reserved to ask any questions. No matter how many times I asked, no one had a comment or thought to share. Trying to talk about the socioeconomic aspects of community health seemed futile with such a stoic group, so I spent the morning doing a quick review of treatment guidelines for diarrheal illnesses. After lunch we did some role-playing, with each participant playing a patient or a health worker. Those playing the health workers had to think critically about a problem and come to some logical treatment decision. I intended the exercise to be humorous as well as educational, but the women seemed self-conscious about having to act. In general, I was happy with how much they knew, though a few of the older workers led the group in making treatment decisions. After a tea break, I discussed some basics about the science of epidemiology (the study of disease in populations), the usefulness of making maps of disease incidence in a community, and the concept of community diagnosis. They listened, although I don't know how much they took in. We finished early, and they filled out questionnaires about our first day together. All of the workers gave my class an excellent rating, but they felt I had done too much lecturing, which was true enough.

The next day was similar. I tried various teaching methods to engage the health workers, but the young women were too demure for lively discourse. They seemed to prefer sitting passively, soaking in as much as I was physically able to feed them. Delek Hospital's new community health worker, Lhamo, who had been educated in the U.S., finally managed to goad them into making posters and puppets. They were reluctant at first, but came to enjoy the exercise. One older health worker even made a cardboard "Chain of Disease" based on concepts I had taught the day before. I was pleased to have proof that someone had been listening. After class they apparently complained that I did too much lecturing.

When the second batch of health workers arrived, I was surprised to see two men among them. Some of the workers were from southern settlements and had journeyed 2 to 3 days to get to Dharamsala. Overall, these workers seemed older and more experienced than those in the previous group, but I found out that they were equally reticent to speak. It was like pulling teeth to get them to speak up, to say anything forceful, or to express their opinion. I understood that in some cultures challenging a teacher is not routinely done as it is considered to be disrespectful.

In the morning I discussed how to diagnose specific diseases, how to ask the right questions, how to recognize the stages of dehydration. They didn't say a word, except when I told them not to give loperamide or other commonly sold gut relaxants. They liked to use those with their patients. After lunch we tried some role-playing, but they were too reserved to engage even with the Tibetan instructor. On the topic of the social causes of disease, they seemed fairly astute, just not zealous. I hoped they left with the idea that they could be both diagnosticians and health advocates for their communities.

I learned a few lessons from this training on water-borne diseases that I would take with me in future lessons. First, relating to the trainee on his or her level is important. Without that 1-to-1 relationship, learning will not happen. Second, the easy method of lecturing without interacting is not the best learning method. Even though many children grow up this way, their intuition can be unlocked if they are given the chance. Third, applying the principle of equity in community health education is important. Everyone, no matter their level of education or understanding, should be given access to the same health information and services that can make a difference in their lives. Applying education discriminatingly to a distinct population can only lead to a perception of imbalance. Fourth, integrating education around curative medicine and preventive medicine is the best way to get those messages of prevention out there. Many people want to know about their present health problems in the here and now, before learning about how to prevent problems in the future. Lastly, empowering people through putting knowledge in their hands and teaching them how to use it is the best skill an educator can give.

I spent the following Saturday at the Tibetan Children's Village with a group of foreigners who wanted to play soccer, or "football" as it is called in most regions of the world. Jean-Claude talked some monks from the nearby monastery of the Dalai Lama into opposing us, and we met at the school's dusty field, which was a full playing field complete with goal posts. Our ragtag team of foreigners was made up of four Frenchmen, four Israelis that we pulled off the street, a Belgian, a Canadian, a New Zealander, and me. Most of us had never met before. We barely had time for proper introductions before the monks came strolling onto the field. In unison, they threw off their robes to reveal flashy maroon spandex pants and team T-shirts. I thought they would look great in a television ad back home. We were sure we'd get stomped.

The first half ended 2-2, with the foreigners totally winded. Most of the game had been played entirely on our end of the field. The team of monks probably had 12 shots on goal to our four. We begged for a longer halftime, blaming the altitude for our state of exhaustion, but the winter sun was heading west. We did a little better in the second half. With 5 minutes left, we got a long ball down to their end in front of the goalie. In the ensuing scuffle, the ball popped out in front of me, and I booted it in. We were tied 4-4. Time ended, and I voted for a draw. I thought this would go over especially well with the monks, given their Buddhist philosophy of harmony and loving kindness. To the contrary, they wanted to play to sudden death, winner take all. Five minutes into overtime, with us foreigners lethargically walking the field in our fatigue, the team of spirited monks in spandex finished us off 5-4. What ever happened to the Buddhist eternal wheel of compassion? I surmised it did not apply to all things, especially football. I could barely walk the next day, my muscles ached so badly.

Back at work, we faced another outbreak of unknown cause, this time involving workers at the Dalai Lama's reconstructed Norbulingka Palace. The typical history was a few days of fevers and headaches, but no flu-like symptoms, rash, cough, diarrhea, or signs of urinary tract infections or meningitis. Chest x-rays were clear, malaria smears negative; there were no physical findings except fevers. We were baffled. Our first group of possible diseases included typhoid, malaria, influenza, and hepatitis. Our second group included diseases less likely to occur but certainly possible in India, including leptospirosis (bacteria spread by rats), brucellosis (bacteria spread through unpasteurized milk), typhus, and dengue fever (virus carried by mosquitoes). Since we couldn't test reliably for any of those in our hospital's laboratory, we just had to watch and wait. All the workers ended up recovering without treatment, and the outbreak ceased as quickly as it had started, leaving the entire hospital staff puzzled.

At the same time, we began seeing a lot of students from Sogar School with everything from amoebic dysentery to typhoid. The school's jeep was now mainly used to bring sick students to Delek Hospital. I asked Jean-Claude to accompany me on a site visit to find out what might be making so many students ill. We did a thorough inspection of the grounds and living conditions, making detailed notes on what we found.

The students' diet seemed adequate, though the cooks boiled the vegetables too long, ensuring a thorough leaching of vitamins. The students did not have fruit on a regular basis, and more troubling, there was no boiled water in the kitchen for drinking. A small stream running through the camp had a pipe hooked up for hand washing, but many of the students used this untreated water for drinking and brushing their teeth as well. This water was surely unfit to drink.

The latrines were, as we expected, quite unhygienic. In addition, the women's latrine lacked a tap with running water, soap for washing, a space for bathing, a light, doors on the stalls, and a hygienic environment in general. The men's latrine was 100 meters away and even dirtier. The men had a tap, but no shower or bathing area. Their water pipe actually ran right past the women's latrine, but did not stop. For bathing, the students used a nearby river with no provisions for privacy. The women spoke of local Indians staring at them while they bathed, a problem that surely contributed to their poor hygiene.

The school only had generator power – 1 hour in the morning and 2 hours at night. There were one or two lights in each dormitory, to serve two or three dozen students. The strain on their eyes had to be enormous. Overcrowding was a problem, with the bunks pushed close together; the students were packed in like proverbial sardines. It was surprising we had not seen more TB at the camp.

The biggest concern by far, as I had noted on previous visits, was that Sogar School had no consistent source of potable water. The water designated for drinking was piped in from a nearby village, but the sample Jean-Claude tested had more than 10 coliform colonies per 100 ml (a normal level is less than 1 colony per 100 ml). Coliforms are bacteria that cause diarrhea. It was thus no mystery why so many students were showing up at the hospital with diarrhea. The only good thing about the water was a high level of natural fluoride, which protected the students from tooth decay. We delivered our findings and specific recommendations to the Tibetan Home Department, which was responsible for Sogar School. They took our suggestions seriously and began making plans for some improvements.

In the meantime, it was my turn to visit another site that was in dire need of attention, the Elders Home. This time, I invited my Tibetan teacher to come along as a translator. I had already written several letters to the Home Department, suggesting things that could be improved. The three biggest needs were a competent translator, a reliable system for supplying the patients' medications, and someone to make sure the patients were taking their medications properly. A community health worker would have fit all three bills, but the Home Department had refused our first request.

Having my teacher along as a translator meant I could talk to the geriatric patients this time, instead of trying to guess at their conditions. More importantly, I could explain what I thought was wrong and recommend treatments, instead of just handing over a prescription. I was finally able to get the old man with the terrible cough to agree to a chest x-ray. I was able to check the electrolytes of several patients with diabetes and hypertension. And I got to have a conversation with the schizophrenic nun who wandered in and out of clinic each week. I could hardly believe how much I accomplished. Simply being able to communicate made all the difference in the world, and I immediately wrote again to the Home Department to say so.

By mid-winter, the patient load at the hospital had grown considerably lighter. I had expected the harsh weather to bring more patients, but the opposite was true. Probably those with minor illnesses didn't want to make the trip in the cold. We were now seeing 15 to 20 patients in clinic each morning instead of 30, so I could take 10 minutes per person instead of 6. It was more manageable, but if someone had told me while I was still in my Western residency training program that I would soon be seeing 20 patients in one morning, I would have laughed.

It was a good thing the patient load was shrinking, because the hospital was once again short-staffed. Susan's term was up (she had been there for 6 weeks, but had largely kept to herself), and a few weeks would elapse before any new volunteers arrived. That left just me and a British couple with a 10-month-old baby. Michael and Victoria were both doctors, but only one could work at any given time while the other looked after Emma. They were also both general practitioners, and had decided to move to Dharamsala and volunteer for 1 year before opening up their own practice in England. I was impressed with their service ethic, and the fact that they brought along their young child. Unlike many physicians with an interest in international public health, Michael and Victoria wanted to live and work in the same place day after day for an extended period, as opposed to those spending only a few days or weeks in a country. It's often the latter that get the "guts and the glory," flying into crisis situations and doing high profile humanitarian work that dramatically saves lives. We were saving lives at Delek Hospital as well, although the work was seldom if ever acknowledged.

One day, Michael came running out of his room exclaiming that Emma had said her first real word, "Buddha!" I didn't believe him until I heard it with my own ears. It was a fitting and appropriate word for the start of Michael's career, given the setting.

With fewer patients being admitted, we had a little more free time in the afternoons. On the evening of the next full moon, I decided to hike up to Triund (9,500 feet) with some other foreigners. The plan was to hike with the full moon lighting our way, but it didn't quite work out that way. The moon was not yet up when the sun went down, so we found ourselves halfway up the hill in the dark. We stumbled the rest of the way with flashlights, and eventually reached the plateau where others had already lit a campfire. The full moon finally rose, and its projection on the Dhauladhar Range was beautiful, glowing, and evanescent. Fifteen of us camped out in the lodge, ate rice and *dal*, drank Scotch whiskey brought by a visiting doctor from Scotland, and sang some old songs around the campfire.

Unfortunately I was on call the next day. I woke up at dawn and jogged down the hill in freezing weather to make it back to the hospital by 9 a.m. It was the busiest call day in a while. I must have seen about 40 patients in the morning session. A few had minor skin infections, but most had colds or the flu (no one got flu shots that year because they were too costly). Then came a case that illustrated to me just how poor some of the refugees were. The patient was a young mother with a severe breast infection. She had been in a few days earlier, but had not bought the prescribed amoxicillin because she could not afford it. The 7-day regimen would have cost about $3. Now she was so sick, she had to be admitted.

Over lunch, I paid a house call to a private patient with atrial fibrillation and congestive heart failure. The man was too weak to leave his house, so I brought refills of his medications. Despite being quite poor, his family graciously offered me tea and powdered sugar pastries. It was all I had time to eat that afternoon, and I was very grateful.

When I returned to the hospital, two Austrians came in and asked me to write letters declaring that they had amoebic dysentery, so they could extend their visas. It seemed like a bit of truth-stretching that would harm no one, and I was going to do it, but another staff doctor advised me not to. Earlier in the month, the police had come by while I was out to take down the names of the hospital's foreign volunteers, because we were technically working in India illegally. If we started getting into the habit of extending visas by issuing fake certificates, the Foreigners Registration Office might crack down on the volunteers. I had to refuse.

The highlight of the day came in the afternoon when Tenzin came in for a checkup for his TB meningitis. It was a gratifying moment. Almost all of his left-side weakness had resolved. Seeing Tenzin, even if it was during the busiest of days, never failed to cheer my spirits.

In the late evening, just as I was preparing to listen to the BBC news on my shortwave radio, a man turned up asking for a full physical exam. He needed a medical certificate for a job application, and it was due the next day. It seemed inconsiderate that he would show up at night with such a request, but we were accustomed used to being called upon at all hours. I asked him why he had not come in earlier, but he just muttered that he'd had work to do. He told me he had no major medical problems, so I agreed to do the physical. It didn't take me long to discover a respiratory rattle all the way up and down the right side of his chest. Only then did he admit that he was a TB patient! I felt this was a bit audacious. I told him he couldn't have a medical certificate until he got a chest X-ray, which he would have to wait until morning to receive.

When I returned to Sogar School the following week, I could hardly believe how many improvements had been made since Jean-Claude and conducted our site visit. It seemed each of the points in our report was being addressed one by one. The Home Department had hired a contractor to build a small bridge over the stream, had asked the local authority to lay cables to bring electricity to the school, and had set aside some money to construct a small shower building for the camp's building. The camp administrative staff were following our instructions as well. They had stopped boiling the vegetables so long, and were planning to buy enough fruit in the spring for a daily portion per student.

Most importantly, I found that the school's health worker had started chlorinating the water – true progress! Lobsang had attended the water-borne disease course and learned from Jean-Claude how to calculate the volume of a water tank and how much chlorine to add. No wonder it had been a few weeks since we had seen any Sogar School students with typhoid or amoebic dysentery. I felt a strong sense of accomplishment in being part of a group effort that had brought about such a verifiable improvement in the students' health. Teamwork had translated into measurable enhancements in the quality of life for these newly arrived refugees. My only hope was that conditions at the camp would continue to improve over the months to come.

Circumnavigating Buddhist temples and spinning their prayer wheels is a regular ritual for Tibetans, even for those disabled.

Tradtional female Tibetan dancers performing in Dharamsala.

Thangka painting of Buddhist images is a craft reserved for
only the most skilled Tibetan painters.

A private audience with the Dalai Lama is one benefit of serving at Delek Hospital. Also pictured is Ms. Elizabeth Fabel.

Tibetan monks gathering for a rally for His Holiness the Dalai Lama.

This elderly Tibetan woman was always happy to share a smile.

7

Hard Lessons

As winter pushed on, the days became short, dark, and wet. Daytime temperatures hovered around 30 degrees Fahrenheit, with freezing rain that persisted for weeks. All I could do to keep warm was stay inside my small room in the hospital and crank up the little coil floor heater as high as it would go. The large windows in my room with the beautiful views of the Indian Gangetic Plain had now become a liability, letting the heater's warm air leak out as quickly as it was produced. At least the patient load remained relatively light, and the hospital now had six doctors, making it possible for us to take on some additional responsibilities.

One of our new work rotations was at the Tibetan Medical and Astrological Institute, where we took turns going on rounds with the traditional Tibetan doctors. It was a task I looked forward to with plenty of curiosity and a modicum of doubt. Several very ill patients had recently been transferred from the Institute to Delek Hospital for intensive care, so I suspected that the rounds were meant to assist the Tibetan doctors rather than to educate the foreign physicians about Tibetan medicine. To their credit, the traditional Tibetan physicians probably knew more about the practice of allopathic medicine than we did about traditional Tibetan medicine.

Rounds at the Institute were less formal and more pleasant than at Delek. The inpatient ward was much nicer than ours, with real tile rather than cement and a bright and cheery atmosphere. On the first day I participated in the Institute's medical rounds, there was only one female patient. She was a Sogar School student, whose complaints included burning on urination, headache, muscle aches, and absence of menstruation. I had been asked to look in on her to try to make a diagnosis. I had heard that she had been sterilized in Tibet, something I was unable to verify with the diagnostic tools we had at our disposal. The only proper method would have been to inject dye into the female reproductive tract, to make sure it would flow backward all the way to the ovaries. I suspected a urinary tract infection and would have treated her with antibiotics, but the Tibetan doctors seemed satisfied that she was doing better with their drugs. I didn't object much, as she was not seriously ill.

The male patients were much less interesting. One had just left Delek, where we had diagnosed him with hepatitis (liver inflammation) caused by the hepatitis A virus. Another had gastritis-like symptoms, and a third complained of neck pain. As I was leaving, a friend of the monk with gastritis asked me how I would treat the condition. I suggested acid blockers, and privately wondered if the monk was unhappy with the treatment he was receiving at the Institute. In the end, our short rounds provided only limited opportunities to learn Tibetan medicine. It was probably too short a visit for the doctors to explain the nuances of such a complicated system. Tibetan medicine was touted as more effective than Western drugs for some chronic ailments, I had yet to see a "randomized controlled" clinical study demonstrating that fact. All we had to go on was anecdotal evidence and patient reports, which deserved some credence in the absence of scientific trials.

In a broader sense, none of the Delek doctors doubted the role that Tibetan medicine played in the exile community. Medical systems, as they modernize, become wedded to the large community discourse on ethnic and political nationalism, the political rights of indigenous people, and the role and authority of biomedicine. Contemporary medicine has become, to the lay Tibetan public, a font of ethnic revitalization and resistance to the modernization policies of the Chinese state. Tibetan medicine represents a public context where Tibetan ideas about the body-mind connection, social ethics, and the health consequences of modernity can be freely expressed. This process is no more evident than in the elaboration of disorders of *rlung*, discussed in the previous chapter, a class of illness that collectively has come to symbolize the suffering inherent in rapid, social, and economic change.

From a public health perspective, the "epidemiologic transition" theory hypothesizes that societies develop from times of pestilence and famine to a period when infectious diseases cause the largest amount of mortality and morbidity, and then further to an era of degenerative man-made diseases. In this era, indigenous medical practice such as Tibetan medicine is thought to play a more pronounced role. Most developing countries, however, face an increasing burden of disability from chronic disease while at the same time suffering from continued high rates of infectious disease. In this transformation, which had already hit India, indigenous medicine will be asked to play a larger role. Despite the striking differences from the Western paradigm, I developed a great respect for traditional Tibetan medicine. I still feel that integrating both traditions in a complimentary manner has the most to offer patients.

After the rounds, I had lunch with a Russian man who was studying Tibetan medicine at the Institute. He was from the Russian province of Kalmichia, just west of the Central Asian country of Kazakhstan. He had been studying urology in Russia, but when funding from his province dried up, he decided to study Tibetan medicine instead. Oddly enough, he was convinced this was going to allow him to make a comfortable living back in his province.

That afternoon was the premier showing of a film called "Tears of Torture" by Ngawang Dorjee, the young and humble photographer for the Tibetan Government-in-Exile. He filmed interviews with two Dolma Ling nuns who had survived imprisonment and torture in Tibet. One of the women had been sexually assaulted with an electric cattle prod. Both nuns were at the premier in person, though they held their heads down during most of the 30-minute documentary.

After the viewing, I asked the director about his plans for the film. Much to my surprise, he replied that he had none. I suggested he try to get some publicity. "The film is very good," I told him. "It's rare to see nuns talk on camera about being tortured in Tibet. It could help the Tibetan cause if the international community hears about their experiences." I added that I would try to locate a public program in the U.S. that might broadcast the film.

My next call day started off with antenatal clinic – measuring bellies and prescribing iron-folate to pregnant mothers. Standard "bread and butter" general practice medicine. The real challenge came at lunchtime, when I admitted a Greek dharma student with severe jaundice. His complexion was as yellow-orange as a summer squash and he had been having fevers for about a week. Our labs ruled out the obvious suspect, hepatitis, but found his bilirubin was a whopping 21 milligrams per deciliter.[13]

The problem was that our blood chemistry machine couldn't differentiate between indirect bilirubin (from the destruction of blood cells) or direct bilirubin (from a liver or gall bladder disease). To me, given the context in which his disease started, some type of obstruction in his gallbladder system seemed most likely. The man was in his late 30s, slightly overweight, and a bit of a drinker, so liver disease was also a possibility. I put him on oral antibiotics, intravenous fluids, and medicine for his hiccups. He initially perked up and was quite alert by the evening. In retrospect, I should have realized that he was sicker than he looked, much more so.

The following morning, the patient was in a stupor. His sudden change in mental status combined with his jaundice suggested probable brain encephalopathy (or coma) as a complication of liver disease. The puzzling thing was that his liver function appeared normal. Michael and I discussed the possibility of inflamed bile ducts, but we didn't have the right medicines and/or technology to treat that in our remote hospital. Considering his poor status, we decided to transfer him to the nearest tertiary care teaching hospital in Chandigarh, 6 hours away.

One of the staff doctors volunteered to take the patient and his girlfriend in the hospital's diesel station wagon. As they wound their way along the bumpy roads of Himachal Pradesh, the patient became more and more stuporous, then finally became unconscious. The emergency ward doctors in Chandigarh treated him for several hours, but he was too ill for them to intervene in time. He died at midnight. The probable cause of death was disseminated intravascular coagulation, or DIC, the formation of small blood clots throughout the

---

[13] A normal bilirubin is below 3.0 milligrams per deciliter.

body, which can use up the blood's clotting factors and cause severe bleeding. The condition was probably triggered by the patient's high levels of liver bilirubin. I had seen people die from DIC in Cambridge, but it was usually possible to replace the blood's clotting agents through a plasma transfusion.

The next morning, the man's girlfriend came back to Dharamsala. She took the bad news surprisingly well. "It was part of his karma," she told me. "He had predicted he was going to die and he was ready for it."

"What about you?" I asked.

"I was ready, too. There were several signs that this would happen. The number on his hospital bed was my birthday, and the number on his room was my birth month. Also, the other doctors have a baby named Emma, the same name as my sister."

"I would call those coincidences."

"They were signs," she insisted.

To some extent I felt the same as she did – that death is a part of everyday life, and when it comes we shouldn't be so surprised. Any of us could go at any moment. This was quite apparent now in my sixth month of volunteer medical work in a low-resource setting. But it was tough knowing that this man had died in his 30s from a condition we could have treated in the U.S. One thing was certain – I was glad I had my evacuation insurance in case such a thing ever happened to me.

The man's death was the main topic of discussion at our physicians' meeting Monday morning. The hospital director, Dr. Tsetan, asked us to reflect on what more we could or should have done.

"An ultrasound would have been helpful," Michael suggested. "But we can only get them sporadically at the Zonal Hospital. When we do, the readings are often unintelligible."

"I should have put him on intravenous antibiotics instead of oral," I said. "He just didn't look so sick when he came in. The jaundice could have been from a simple case of hepatitis A, and we were only able to rule that out after his labs came back. I think the real problem was a bad infection in his gallbladder duct. Maybe intravenous antibiotics would have cleared it up, but the prognosis would have been poor even in the best tertiary care hospital."

"What about the medicine you gave him for hiccups?" Dr. Tsetan asked.

"It can make people sleepy and would have built up in someone with liver failure, but that's not what killed him."

Dr. Tsetan wasn't convinced. "How will it look for the hospital if someone finds out? What if one of his relatives decides to sue the hospital?"

Though I could not tell if he was asking a rhetorical question, I suddenly realized that he felt I was partly to blame for the death. It shocked me into silence. Bryan, one of the newest volunteers, saw my reaction and spoke up. "In the off chance that a case like this ever goes to court, would you stick up for us?" Dr. Tsetan had trouble composing his reply and I couldn't tell if he said yes or no. I went away from our medical rounds that morning with the impression of Dr. Tsetan as a worried leader with difficult choices to make that were often in conflict. He seemed torn between supporting his volunteer, expatriate staff and preserving the life of his small yet vital hospital. None of us were working in India legally (all were on tourist visas), and thus had no practice insurance. Though I did not fault him for his position, I felt unnerved for many days afterward. The event was a bonding moment for us volunteer physicians, and we made an attempt to support each other and discuss cases with each other more often.

The most moving moment of this whole story came when the patient's girlfriend was preparing to leave. "I just wanted to thank you again," she said. "It was so thoughtful when you told us to ask for sterile needles in the lab. I want you to know how much I appreciate the concern you've shown throughout all this." She decided to donate 2,000 rupees (about $65 at the time) to Delek Hospital and wanted to know how it should be used.

"Sterile needles and gloves," I replied. I was stunned, and of course, grateful. Sterile needles were always in short supply. The nurses typically sterilized needles for reuse in an autoclave machine, which was not adequate for killing viruses like hepatitis B or HIV. The hospital administrator felt the cost of buying new needles and syringes for each patient was just too costly, despite the risk of

HIV/AIDS and hepatitis transmission. He suggested we throw away the needles and reuse the syringes, but we had no way to keep the syringes sterile.

Disposal of the needles was another big problem at the hospital. When I first arrived, used needles and syringes were tossed in the general garbage bin. Our garbage handlers, Indian women of low caste, then took the bins out barehanded to a bin hole in the ground across the street. Every now and then, a truck came by and hauled the bins away. Now at least we had a needle/sharps bin to keep the hazardous waste separate from the rest of the trash. But we hadn't figured out what to do with the bins full of needles. They needed to be buried, but where?

The following week, Michael admitted a monk who had developed swelling and pain after bumping his right thigh on a table. Michael was convinced it was a blood clot, or deep vein thrombosis, and put him on heparin. By the time I came on call, the patient had been on heparin for about a week, but his leg was getting worse not better. The bump looked and felt hard, and I suspected a deep abscess even though there was no redness or inflammation. Everyone thought I was foolish when I said I was going to stick a needle into his thigh to figure out what exactly was going on inside. I went ahead, despite the other volunteers' objections. One stick with the needle and we got a diagnosis: the most copious, free-flowing, putrid pus I had ever seen, or smelled. The smell was enough to turn the stomach of even the heartiest physician.

We scheduled the monk for minor surgery, with four doctors and a dentist present to witness the procedure and help with our intravenous anesthesia with the drug named ketamine. Inducing anesthesia with an intravenous drug is more risky than doing it with a gas, but we had neither the proper equipment nor the technical personnel to use gas anesthesia. Ketamine has the advantage of inducing an anesthetic state in the patient at low dose without suppressing the drive to breath, thus the patient does not require assistance from a mechanical ventilator. It is a tricky drug to work with, however, because if you give too much you can actually suppress respiration.

Using ketamine always requires several persons to watch over the patient.

When we finally had the patient in a deep sleep, we began. As soon as I made a small incision, the pus came roaring out. What seemed an entire liter of fluid flowed out of his leg, down a drape, onto the bed, and into a bucket. We must have let it drain for 15 minutes, squeezing out more and more. At one point, pus actually squirted onto Michael's shoes. He was so amazed at the huge amount of pus that we removed, his jaw went slack. As for the monk, he was very lucky. He had been on the verge of getting very, very sick.

Next, Bryan was the one to solve a minor medical mystery. His case was a gem – a chubby-faced, 10-year-old Indian girl, who had been diagnosed with a seizure disorder and put on an anticonvulsant called phenytoin. She had recently had a CT scan, which supposedly showed calcified nodules in her brain. She was put on TB medicine for the nodules and sent on her way. When her parents brought her to Delek, she had been feeling confused for about a week and had become progressively more disoriented until she was unable to walk. Bryan's quick mind figured out that the TB medicine was slowing down the little girl's ability to metabolize her phenytoin. She had become phenytoin toxic. After concluding that her CT scan did not look suggestive of TB, we took her off all of her medications. She was able to walk again a day and a half later. It was just the sort of case that reminded me how important it was to take enough time with each patient. If there hadn't been time to learn the little girl's history and apply some critical thinking, the outcome might not have been so positive.

A few days later, I admitted a young Tibetan woman who complained of breathlessness. She said that she'd had "some kind of heart problem" since she was a girl. I tried to remember all the standard cardiac symptom questions I learned during residency. It seemed like she had all of them.

"When do you feel short of breath?" I asked.

"Anytime I exercise, doctor, or go up the stairs, or do anything with effort," she replied, a bit meekly.

"Are you short of breath at night?"

"Not always. But sometimes I suddenly get short of breath, and have to sit up and wait a while to catch my breath."

There was a name for that, but it was escaping me at present. I later looked it up – paroxysmal nocturnal dyspnea – or the unpredictable shortness of breath that happens at night.

"That must be uncomfortable. Can you lie down flat?" I asked with some trepidation. Her case was beginning to sound more serious, especially for a young person.

"I usually sleep with pillows holding me up. If I don't, I start feeling my heart beat heavy, and it skips beats."

I did a thorough cardiac exam and, to my amazement, discovered the strongest palpable heart pulsation that I had ever felt, as well as a gigantic murmur during the contraction of the heart. In fact, she had a murmur during heart relaxation as well, and a pulse of 180. Her heart murmurs were so loud that you could actually hear them simply by putting the naked ear to the chest. I quickly ordered an EKG and chest X-ray, and found she also had fluid in her lungs, likely backed up from her heart failure. Apparently a cardiologist had put her on a diuretic 4 years ago to prevent this type of accumulation, but it was unclear whether she had been taking the medication regularly. We gave her one dose of furosemide, a particularly powerful diuretic. She was exquisitely sensitive to the drug, and to our relief, she urinated about six times before midnight. It was a fascinating case, and I felt a sense of satisfaction at being able to help her out of her acute state. What she really needed, however, was a mitral valve replacement. We sent her off to a cardiac surgeon, hoping she would somehow be able to afford the operation. If not, she faced certain death in a few short years. I was sad that I could not follow up on her condition. Patients like her were hard to forget.

While fulfilling my clinical obligations, I continued to look for ways to promote health education and human rights among the Tibetan refugee community. Toward the end of December, I finally had the opportunity to meet Ngawang Rabten, the new officer on the Tibetan Human Rights Desk. He had earned a master's degree in International Relations and Human Rights from Columbia University, one of the premier places to study human rights in the U.S. For the past month, he had been in Nepal raising funds for the Human Rights Desk's new computer, which apparently was not in the Tibetan government's budget. At any rate, I hoped to help him tighten up the human rights updates and start compiling information on access to health care inside Tibet. The data were scarce, but troubling stories leaked out from behind the Chinese "red curtain" now and then. In one story we heard, a Lhasa hospital refused to admit a woman in labor until she paid a deposit for the delivery costs. Her husband, a police officer, ran home to get the money. When he returned, he found that his wife had given birth on the front steps of the hospital and had then died, along with the baby. In a rage, the police officer had taken out his pistol, walked into the hospital, shot five or six doctors and the clerk who denied them entry, and killed himself. The story cast doubt on the Chinese government's claim that Tibetans had access to free health care just like any other Chinese citizen.

Another human rights concern that had captured my attention was closer to home. In the community of Dharamsala, as well as across India, young children were employed in homes and businesses by families not related to them. What surprised me, however, was that Tibetan families were doing this also. India had a law against child labor, of course, but it was not well enforced. Most of the child laborers were from the very poor state of Bihar. In exchange for a monthly sum, parents sent their children to live with families in distant cities for one or more years. These children usually did not get to go to school, because they were too busy doing child care and cooking or cleaning. There were many instances of this practice in our town, especially among wealthier Tibetan families and restaurant owners, who recognized that children were cheaper and more malleable than their adult employees.

The Bihari children were rather handsome kids. They spoke English well and often delighted foreigners with their impressive work ethic and flamboyant style as waiters. Their charm helped mask the fact that they were basically indentured servants. This type of arrangement was clearly a violation of international human rights treaties. Article 32 of the Convention on the Rights of the Child encourages countries to "recognize the right of the child to be protected from economic exploitation and from performing any work that is likely to be hazardous or to interfere with the child's education."[14]

Some Tibetans countered this moral argument with a practical one, claiming that the children benefited from the arrangement. The families they served gave them plenty of food, a nicer home, and better medical care than they received in Bihar. "The use of these children gives them a much better life than they would have had at home," one apologist told me. "You can't apply Western standards of employment here. The situation is just so different."

Those who defended the practice seemed to dismiss the fact that the Bihari children had no say in the matter, were often taken from their families against their will, and were missing out on an education. How could that be in their best interest? Furthermore, the monthly payments due to their parents were often late or never made at all. The children may have been treated well, but that didn't change the fact that they and their families were being exploited. I felt the Tibetan Government-in-Exile could eradicate the practice with a little encouragement, so I decided to send a letter to the Information Department. I wasn't sure I would get a response, but it felt like a good thing to do, particularly on the day before Christmas.

On Christmas Eve, I attended a service at St. John's in the Wilderness, a rundown Scottish Episcopalian chapel on the slope of a hill. There must have been about 100 Westerners there, singing "Silent Night" and thinking of their families at home. Just after Michael and I left, a South African man took a fall outside the church. He had been walking up the hill when a jeep drove past. He jumped out of the way and stumbled over a wall, falling 15 feet straight down onto his back. Nobody at the church wanted to move him, so the man's Italian friend took the jeep to get us at the restaurant (luckily, someone knew where we had gone.) We were sitting

[14] The Convention of the Rights of the Child (CRC) was written and adopted in 1989, and came into force in 1990 when the required number of nations signed and ratified it. All member nation states of the United Nations have signed and ratified the CRC, except for the United States and Somalia (which doesn't have much of a government). The CRC lays out the civil, political, social, economic, and cultural rights of children.

there eating our *palak paneer* when the Italian walked in and said, "Is there anyone here named Tim and Michael?" We rode back with him in the jeep and found that the man was awake, but had not been moved. We talked to him, got him up, determined that he was quite all right, and everyone quickly resumed their Christmas Eve celebrations. We were in such good spirits that we hardly minded when the power went out for most of Christmas Day. Fortunately, it came back on in time for the volunteers to cook up a Western-style Christmas dinner at the hospital: three dressed birds, 6 pounds of potatoes, chutney, salad, and even Christmas cake.

Since I had all of Christmas off, I volunteered to be on call the last day of the year. I spent my New Year's Eve examining the bottom of an elderly woman who complained of blood in her stool. She had a fleshy growth on her rectum the size of an orange – rectal cancer, I assumed. I took her to the Zonal Hospital for a second opinion, but the surgeon there said it was just hemorrhoids. I had never seen anything like it. You know the old adage, that how you spend your New Year's Eve sets the tone for the following year? When I finally got to bed that night with the image of giant hemorrhoids stuck in my mind, I fervently hoped the adage wouldn't prove true for me.

8

Progress

I spent the first day of the New Year doing the same thing I would have been doing in Massachusetts – sledding! The prospects for sledding are not abundant in Dharamsala. Despite the chill at an elevation of 6,000 feet, the community is too close to the equator to sustain winter snowfall. So I planned a day trip to the mountains with seven other volunteers and staff from the hospital. We decided to hike up to Triund, where we had celebrated the last full moon. It took 2 hours to reach the snow line, after which we continued climbing slowly up the steepest part. There were footprints marking the trail, but as the morning wore on, the snow became softer in the sun. Occasionally, I stepped into one of the footprints and sank in up to my thighs. It was a wonderful feeling to be back in snow, reminiscent of my childhood. At the top of the ridge, the snow was more than waist-high, and I quickly found myself coated in snow up to my belt. I couldn't have been happier.

The view from Triund was spectacular, with the whole Dhauladhar Range laid out before our eyes, glistening under white blankets. Many of us would have gone further if possible, but the snow was too deep. It was cold up there, too – below freezing. After a quick lunch of oranges, crackers, and water, Bryan led us in the descent. He jumped off a small cliff and landed on his bottom, then started sliding down the mountain. I was envious of his ski pants – my jeans were cold and soggy. I wasn't prepared to jump off any cliffs, but I followed Bryan down some gentler "runs" and had a blast. The year was off to a good start – not a patient with hemorrhoids in sight.

On the second day of the year, an American relief group showed up to offer free vision exams and glasses to the public. Delek Hospital had received no advance notice, which made it apparent that there would be little or no coöperation between the relief workers and the hospital's staff optician. I had sent several patients to get glasses at our eye clinic, and the optician seemed to do a good job. So I was surprised to see a relief group coming to deliver what was already available. Would the group offer anything we couldn't provide?

The workers set up their project on the patio of the Dalai Lama's monastery, and I walked up to have a look. It was a cold, sunny day, and the patio was crowded with disorderly Tibetans and Indians waiting to be seen. I counted about 200 persons. Norbu, a monastery secretary, switched easily between Tibetan, Hindi, and English, as he tried to control the crowd. Norbu was the monk in charge of receiving foreign guests at the monastery. He even had a photo with Tibet supporter Harrison Ford hanging on his wall.

As I watched from the sidelines, a young man with curly brown locks came up behind me. He was dressed in Seattle grunge, and said he had come to preach the gospel of Jesus. A Christian evangelist in the seat of Tibetan Buddhism? I turned away from him.

After about 10 minutes, a friendly-faced woman from the eye service strolled by, noticed me, and asked, "Oh, are you just passing through India?"

"No, I actually live and work here," I responded. *You're the one just passing through*, I wanted to say, but didn't. I told her I wanted to talk about ophthalmology with the group's doctors, so she led me through the throngs to the exam room.

It turned out that there were no ophthalmologists. The volunteers were all opticians, there only to check vision. Evaluating cataracts, glaucoma, and the need for surgery and other procedures was out of their league. Seeing that the four opticians were busy fitting glasses, I went back outside and ran into two of the volunteers who had just been to Delek Hospital for a tour. They told me the group of 20 had come from Volunteer Optometric Services to Humanity International (VOSH). They were on a 2-week tour of India, with stops to do vision checks and fittings in four cities. Most of the volunteers were from Missouri and Arkansas, and at least half were along "just for the ride" – to see India and do crowd control. One of the women asked me bluntly about Delek Hospital's attitude toward their operation. Apparently one of my volunteer physician colleagues had told her it was a shame VOSH hadn't coördinated its efforts with Delek Hospital and its staff.

"I hear some of you aren't thrilled with our project," she said. "Do you all feel that way?"

"Well, Delek Hospital, as part of its primary care mission to the Tibetan refugee community, provides the same eye services you're here to offer," I told her. "Our optician does exams and fits glasses, all at a minimal cost to the local community. You're duplicating those services. Granted, you're able to see a large number of patients at once, but it would have been nice to coöperate with us. I'm sure our optician would have appreciated some refresher training too."

My remarks stunned her; she fell silent.

"When foreigners come in with big, highly publicized, short-term projects, the results can actually hurt the Tibetans in the long run," I explained. "It creates dependency on the West. Tibetans already have the belief that foreigners, particularly Americans and Europeans, do things better than they do. They tend to think, 'Anything foreign must be good.' Having more foreign relief projects, instead of developing locally based projects, encourages the Tibetans to rely on these kinds of things. It reminds me of the old proverb of giving someone a fish to eat, versus teaching someone to fish for their food. I think it would have been better to put the money into the Delek Hospital Eye Clinic, to expand and inspire trust in a Tibetan-run operation. In a way you are undermining the local services."

The Tibetan eye clinic was not a full service ophthalmology clinic, but it served the needs of the refugee community pretty well. It was a one room operation, with an optometrist staff person and a good collection of eyeglasses that patients could choose from. Our optometrist was a quiet, capable young woman, and I often wondered if we kept her busy enough with referrals to her service. The community seemed to know about her, but the clinic was not often busy. I was curious to know more.

Another problem I saw with the VOSH program was that it was essentially relief work. What the Tibetans really needed was sustainable development work – the creation of programs that would serve people year-round, not just for 3 days. Sustainable development is a concept from the early 1980s, when it was first used in the

Brundtland Commission report of the United Nations. It was defined as development that met immediate human needs while preserving the natural environment, so that needs can be met not only in the present but also in the future. It's development that does not compromise the ability of future generations to meet their own needs. As I saw it, VOSH was compromising the future development of optometry in Dharamsala with their relief visit. Relief work has its place in disaster management, but not in the peaceful, long-established community of Dharamsala. Anything short of a lasting commitment to improving the lives of the local population is sometimes called "medical tourism," done more for your own benefit than for the residents'.

My views were relayed to the group's guide, a woman from Wisconsin who lived in Dharamsala part of the year. "How can you criticize what we're doing? We're reaching people who never would be reached," she railed at me. "We're helping people who never would be helped. Our volunteers spent a lot of money to come here."

I could barely get a word in edgewise. "All I'm suggesting is that some coöperation would have—"

"We're happy to coöperate," she insisted. "Once we've finished with all the exams, we'll give you a list of those who need cataract surgery. Then you can follow up and make sure they are treated." She hadn't even considered that we already had our own list, and we were in the process of bringing over an eye surgery team from Washington University.

The leader of the VOSH team, an optician called Dr. Brad, was the next to seek me out. He was excited because he had found an old woman with a tumor on her eye.

"We've known about that for 3 months," I told him, deflating his pride. "She has refused to have surgery."

"I hear you don't approve of our project," he said after a pause.

I could hardly bear having the same argument again. "Do you ever do anything besides one-time clinics?" I asked. "For example, how about holding a training session for local opticians?"

"I tried that once in El Salvador and Nicaragua 15 years ago," he answered. "The problem is you can't get volunteers to live and work in the same place for extended periods. Doctors need excitement. They always want to go someplace new."

I wondered then if they were doing this clinic for the betterment of the Tibetans, or for themselves. He was telling this to me, a doctor who had signed on to spend an entire year in the same place. I didn't feel like arguing any more. I started to walk away.

"We just want to help," he yelled after me. "We're not here to change things."

The trouble was that they were slowly but surely changing things – arguably for the worse. I was certain that many Tibetans participated in the project – whether they were having eye problems or not – just because it was run by foreigners (non-Tibetans and non-Indians). No one wanted to miss out on the "opportunity." While I was watching the patients move through the eye chart station, five people in a row had 20/20 vision. Then I ran into my Tibetan teacher with her mother and one of the nurses from Delek Hospital. "Why did you come?" I asked. "We have a perfectly good eye service at Delek."

With glazed over eyes, they told me the same thing. "These are special doctors from the United States, and they are giving out free glasses." All I could do was sigh.

In the end, 1,500 people showed up for the clinic, reinforcing the relief workers' belief that their services were in dire need. In reality, all of those patients could have been seen at our clinic. While I appreciated that the volunteers had come a long way with the best intentions, I felt frustrated. The group just showed up and held a clinic without any concept of the community's real needs. They never bothered to consider the benefits of working with local services to make them more sustainable and efficient. I couldn't help but conclude that the relief workers were "treating themselves" – making themselves feel good without offering any long-term benefits to the community. That was not team work in my book.

A second source of frustration that first week of the new year was the irregular power supply (or complete lack thereof). Our days and nights became riddled with power cuts, which sometimes lasted as long as 8 hours. You never knew when or where they would strike. The problem was that the hospital was on three different circuits.

Sometimes one side went off, while the others stayed on, then the reverse. This made work extremely difficult, as we could not do labs or X-rays without power. Even when I wasn't working, the outages were maddening. I couldn't use my laptop computer or read a book or cook dinner, and without my electric heater, the room got very cold very quickly. I had to light candles, dress in layers, and wait patiently for the power to return, hoping my body temperature wouldn't drop too much in the meantime.

My own comfort aside, the most frustrating aspect of the power cuts was that the hospital had no generator for the procedure room. We had been asking for a generator for months, but it wasn't in the budget. Once when Michael was on call, a cook from the Tibetan Children's Village came in with severed fingertips. The power was out, so Michael sent him to the Zonal Hospital to see a surgeon. In the late afternoon, the poor man came back to Delek, saying that no one had seen him. He had sat on a bench with his severed fingers for 4 hours, receiving no help at all. At that point, Michael asked me to do anesthesia. We had no general anesthesia equipment and had to use periodic ketamine intravenous injections for any major procedures. The power never came back on, so we worked in a dark operating room. Without a single complaint from the cook, Michael sewed up the man's fingers by the light of a kerosene lamp and candles on the windowsills. It was inspiring.

After reflection, I realized that each of the physicians was adapting to the new climate of practicing medicine in a developing country. Being able to make do with local limitations and changing circumstances is a good trait to have. Although at times we thought we were experiencing the worst conditions possible (sewing up fingers using a kerosene lamp), I'm sure there are other physicians out there practicing in more extreme conditions than we were. In fact, being flexible to change is a very Buddhist trait. For all we knew, we would be here one day, but gone the next. The basic but comfortable conditions I was living and working in were starting to make me less reactionary, more flexible, and less surprised when something I wanted was not available. I was not all that comfortable with that feeling, but I was coping. Having others around to relieve the stress definitely helped. All the volunteer physicians supported each other well. I hoped that I would finally be able to adapt to my surroundings, because the surroundings were unlikely to adapt to my initial needs and expectations. This did not mean giving up on asking for improvements, but just to be more realistic about their chances. Ultimately, I would try to embrace my new environment, as much as it was trying to embrace me.

On the positive side, the new TB plan kicked in at the beginning of January, triggering radical changes in how the disease was treated at Delek Hospital. Now all patients received the same regimen, regardless of the site of infection: four drugs for 2 months, then two drugs for 4 months. It was a regimen called short-course chemotherapy, recommended by the World Health Organization, to standardize how TB was treated worldwide. Previously many hospitals, including our own, had designed their own regimens using a mix-and-match combination of drugs. This new method, called DOTS (for directly observed therapy, short-course), had been shown in studies to cure over 95 percent of patients, and it was easy to use. I was glad our refugee hospital was finally getting on board. Delivering TB medicine through DOTS was the best way to bring down the high rate of TB in the Tibetan community.

In addition, all patients' sputum samples were now to be sent for culture to Cardiff, Wales, in the United Kingdom.[15]

Other changes included a more readable TB reporting form and a policy of keeping all X-rays at the hospital instead of with the patients. Most importantly, the hospital took the humane and wise public health measure of making the medications free for all patients. That naturally meant a huge jump in the cost of the TB program, and its success would depend on increased donations. I wished there also could have been funding for education aimed at slowing the trans-

---

[15] The government of Wales had decided to donate laboratory time and materials to assist Delek Hospital in their TB program. It was of academic interest to the lab as well, because the samples from Delek Hospital patients were more resistant to anti-tuberculosis drugs than any samples collected from Wales. The samples from Delek Hospital were used as "control" samples in their drug-resistance testing. At the time, India had no quality assured laboratory that could do reliable and valid testing of resistance to anti-tuberculosis drugs.

mission of TB. A recent community-wide survey had revealed a variety of misconceptions about the disease. While some respondents were able to name the TB bacillus as the culprit, more than half believed TB was caused by alcohol, poor hygiene, warm weather, mental stress, or eating meat. Educating people about TB was the responsibility of the head nurse who spent time with each patient and his or her family, going over the disease diagnosis, the causative factors, how to treat TB, and how to prevent spreading it to others. With the new program, funds were specifically designated for preparing TB educational materials in Tibetan, a much needed activity.

Before my next visit to Sogar School, I had an idea – I could follow my clinic time there with a health education talk for the students. I went armed with TB flash cards from UNICEF, which one of the health workers had graciously translated from Hindi into Tibetan. After clinic, the students had their afternoon prayer time, an hour of mesmerizing Buddhist chants and meditation. Then we filed into the corrugated tin hall, and I made my presentation. It would have been better to have the students teach themselves instead of listening to a didactic-style lecture, but at least I was able to use flashcards as visual aids. I spoke in English, and Lobsang translated for those who only understood Tibetan.

After some short messages about what causes TB, how it is transmitted, and how it is treated, we opened up a discussion. I was amazed when a few people stuck their hands up immediately and asked some perceptive and insightful questions.

"Why do more Tibetans get TB in India than in Tibet?" one boy asked. "Isn't it because India is warmer?"

I heard this concern all the time. Some Tibetans seemed to believe they were protected against diseases in their homeland and only got TB in India because of the heat. I looked out one of the windows at the dark sky and shivered dramatically.

"It's not hot now, is it?" I asked and got a few laughs. "There is TB in Tibet, too. But the Tibetan settlements in India tend to be very crowded, which helps TB spread quickly from one person to the next through coughing. That's a more likely explanation than the heat."

"Aren't TB drugs very expensive?" another student asked.

"Delek Hospital is in the process of getting funds to provide TB medicines free of charge," I was happy to answer. Providing TB medications free of charge was an essential component of assuring that the poorest refugees finished their entire 6-month course of therapy.

After the half-hour talk was over, the students applauded wildly. It was quite a boost, but I knew that next time I'd have to take a less formal approach. Tibetans were generally apprehensive about sharing their thoughts in front of a room full of their peers. Some of the students felt more comfortable asking their questions privately. Not surprisingly, once the session was over, a few came up and asked questions such as, "Does smoking help TB patients?" and "What are the first signs of TB?"

At the hospital the next morning, a nun from the new arrivals' Reception Center brought in two young monks in training dressed in deep maroon robes. They looked dreadfully ill, with macular red rashes all over their bodies, fever, and cough. I must admit, Choeden the nurse thought of the most likely diagnosis before I did – measles. I had never seen a case before, but sure enough the young boys had the typical spots on their inner cheeks, the most classic sign of measles.[16]

My first thought was to protect all the other kids in the Reception Center from getting exposed. I called the director and asked for isolation for these two patients and vaccinations for the rest. Unfortunately, the Reception Center's health worker had gone south for the Kalachakra Buddhist Initiation festival in the state of Karnataka. Without him, nothing would happen. The boys weren't sick enough to admit, so I gave them some Vitamin A and acetaminophen, arranged to see them the next day, and sent them on their way. I wished I could have done more.

Later that day, Lhamo our community health coordinator returned to work after a prolonged bout with hepatitis B. She had

---

[16] The classic rash on the inside of the mouth and cheeks in persons with measles is known as "Koplik spots."

been out of work for 5 weeks. The fact that a member of the hospital staff had contracted hepatitis B at work made all of us a little nervous. I was convinced that she got the virus from a needle at Delek Hospital, probably during a routine blood test she had from a non-sterile needle. Luckily, we had just received a shipment of hepatitis B vaccine from France, so we began vaccinating the rest of the staff on an accelerated schedule.

The Tibetan holiday known as "Nine Bad Omens" took place the following week. According to legend, at the time of the Buddha one practitioner tried to perform a series of positive actions on this day, and nine bad things happened to him. Consequently, Buddha proclaimed that on this date each year it is best not to try to accomplish much. Tibetans warned us against traveling, working, starting a new project, or going on retreat for at least 24 hours. Traditionally Tibetans play games and have picnics on this day. Some of the hospital's foreign volunteers (myself included) did not heed this warning, and we almost paid a high price.

There had been so many power cuts since the start of the new year that we had trouble keeping track of which of our appliances were on at any given moment. When an outage interrupted your cooking, for example, it was easy to walk away from your stove without remembering to turn it off. When the power came back on, so did the stove – even if the cook was miles away. This is exactly what happened to Bryan and his wife, Nathalie, who decided to start on a 3-day trek up to Kareri Lake during the Nine Bad Omens holiday. Bryan left their electric stove and hot water immersion coil on a wooden stool in their room; apparently he forgot that both were still plugged in when they departed.

When the power came on about 5 hours later, he and Nathalie were well up the hill. The stove and coil burned right through the stool and set fire to the bed and mattress. I was away, but some of the other volunteers soon noticed a burning smell. Michael burst down the door to Bryan's room, and out poured the smoke. He slapped one of his daughter's clean diapers across his mouth, dashed in, and unplugged the appliances. Luckily, the fire had burned itself out.

None of us could figure out how the bed and mattress stopped burning on their own, but we were terribly lucky that the whole hospital hadn't burned down.

Bryan and Nathalie didn't return for another 2 days. In the mean time, I put a sign across their door, "CONDEMNED – by order of the Delek Fire Department, Commissioner I.M. Singed." When they got home, Bryan was so dumbstruck by the event that he kept repeating, "That was damn close." My sentiments exactly. I guess we got off easy considering we had all ignored the warning to keep a low profile during the time of the Nine Bad Omens.

The power cuts continued to grow worse, at one point leaving us in the cold for 2 days straight. With outside temperatures hovering around 30 degrees Fahrenheit, my room reached a low of 45 degrees. Learning the cause of the cuts did nothing to ease my frustration. The Chief Minister of Himachal Pradesh was coming to spend the rest of the winter in Dharamsala, so they had to rewire his colossal Kashmir House. It was like cutting off power to the entire metropolis of Boston, including the hospitals, in order to work on the governor's mansion in Cambridge.

At least the power problems coincided with a continued light patient load, despite it being winter. This gave me the opportunity to talk with some patients at length, even during outpatient clinic, which had been more like an assembly line in the fall. During one of these conversations, I realized that even well educated Tibetans sometimes had a poor understanding of chronic ailments. A good education does not always mean good health literacy, and we had to try to change that.

"I took all my medication, so I should be better," I was told by a government worker whose blood pressure was high. He had taken a single course of anti-hypertensives and expected to be cured.

"High blood pressure isn't like a curable infectious disease, or TB," I explained. "You can't get rid of it. You can only control it. You'll have to take medication for the rest of your life." I prescribed a diuretic and suggested he lose some weight. I also spent some time explaining the basics of hypertension and the importance of maintenance therapy and regular follow-ups. He needed health information in order to play a greater role in taking care of himself.

That afternoon a young woman from the Education Department came in with her husband. She knew English well, but seemed afraid to speak. It turned out she had had no menses for 3 months. She had taken three pregnancy tests without seeing a doctor, and all had come up negative. The couple didn't want a child but wouldn't answer my questions about their use of contraception. The woman felt like she had a gravid uterus to me, and sure enough, this time the pregnancy test came back positive. She decided to have an abortion in the Zonal Hospital, something she probably could have avoided. I was confident this educated young couple knew the basics of family planning, and I began to wonder whether there was some stigma attached to using contraceptives like the birth control pill. One problem was that contraceptives had to be handed out by our chief nurse matron, who was rather strict and preachy.

I would have liked to bring up the topic of birth control at Sogar School, but decided to stick with a more general topic for my next health talk. This time I tried letting the students be their own teachers. We divided them into seven groups and gave each a general question about health, such as "What causes diarrhea?" or "What is TB?" or "What health problems do women have that men don't?" After several minutes of discussion, each group used a microphone to present their responses to the entire school. The answers were all theirs; we didn't facilitate any process at all.

What everyone told me wouldn't work, worked. In the few months since my arrival, I could see that their self confidence had increased dramatically. Not only did we get some of the students to stand up, a few were real hams. One fellow brought down the house with his performances; I felt he had a future as a Tibetan Robin Williams. Overall, their answers were quite good. According to the first group, "Diarrhea is caused by not washing your hands before eating or after the toilet, and eating leftover food." Another group said that good health entails "keeping the environment clean, bathing frequently, washing your clothes, not smoking, and keeping your utensils clean."

A few responses were rather unconventional. For general causes of illness, one group's list included "thinking too much, not following a doctor's advice, and wearing too many clothes." The students also did poorly on a question about TB, despite my presentation the previous week. At least the exercise gave me a good idea of how much they knew and where to start future discussions. The need for women's health education was particularly evident. When asked how to prevent vaginal discharges or infections, the women answered, "Don't have sex, and keep clean."

Continuing the Sogar School health talks on a regular basis would have been optimal, but I did not have the time to prepare lectures or exercises every week. I found out that Delek Hospital's community health nurse had gone to Sogar School twice in the past month to show public health videos. I wondered whether she could take over the responsibility of providing health education for the students. The school's high turnover rate meant a successful program would require frequent repetition of every lesson, for which there was no funding.

On my next visit to Sogar School, a young student came to clinic asking for medication to help his friend.

"Where is he?" I asked.

"In the dormitory," the boy answered. "He can't walk well."

"I'll have to see him before I know what type of medication he needs."

A few minutes later, several boys returned carrying the patient. I quickly realized that he couldn't walk because he had fluid in both knees. I read in his chart that he had been seen for a discharge from his penis, and conjunctivitis during the past 2 weeks. My mind leapt at the possibilities, from septic arthritis to gonorrhea to what I decided in the end was Reiter's Syndrome, a rare rheumatologic problem. I had only seen it once before. The syndrome was originally described during World War I, when a Dr. Reiter noticed soldiers developing swollen joints and conjunctivitis after bouts of bacterial dysentery. It's a fascinating immunologic problem and fairly benign. I prescribed an anti-inflammatory and bed rest and gave the boy a good prognosis.

In mid-January, I had the luck of meeting an American woman who worked with Tibetan refugees in Ladakh, high in the mountains between Kashmir and Tibet. Meredith had some great ideas about health education and had recently started a health project with money from the Canadian government. She used games to convey ideas about hygiene to refugees who bathed once a month and didn't even use water in their compost toilets.

"Ladakh is too cold," she explained. "No one wants to wash."

"How do you manage?" I asked.

"It's cold, but beautiful. Plus the people are wonderful." Meredith had developed a picture book with simple messages about health problems common in Ladakh. Government health officials liked it so much, they asked her to mass-produce it for use in other settlements. The problem was that Ladakh's health issues were not the same as those in the lower altitudes of India, so she needed to incorporate some additional material. That's where I came in. I helped her develop more pages on TB, typhoid, hepatitis, and HIV/AIDS. Meredith had no health training whatsoever, and I couldn't draw worth beans, so we made a perfect team. Once we finished, the picture book was translated by the Health Department and sent to Delhi for printing.

Several months later, I saw a copy of the final book. The quality of the printing was less than optimal, but Meredith's layout was eye-catching and the pictures were well-done and instructive. We were only sent a few boxes of books, which disappeared fast. We didn't have funding to pay for more to be printed. As with many health programs in developing countries, money was the limiting factor. The expertise was there, the heart was there, but the funds were not.

The first big storm of winter coincided with the Indian festival of Lohri, a celebration of winter. Big flakes started falling past my window in the morning. I wanted to see the snowfall in the upper town, so I hiked to McLeod Ganj. It was quite exhilarating to walk straight up a mountain during a snowstorm. The snow kept changing quality as I climbed. By the time I reached the ridge, it was 6 inches deep and still accumulating. I basked in the luxurious, newly fallen flakes. Having grown up in the American Midwest, I have always had a love of snow. Too bad there was nowhere nearby to ski!

As I stood at the McLeod Ganj bus station watching the organized chaos unfold, a shopkeeper, Mr. Nowrojee, invited me into his store. Mr. Nowrojee was the oldest resident of McLeod Ganj and still ran a general store right at the center of town. Folklore had it that it was he who had suggested to the Indian government in 1960 that Dharamsala would be a nice place for the Tibetan refugees to live. At that time, McLeod Ganj was home to little more than his store and a few families. Now it was a crowded mini-metropolis of Tibetans, local Indian businessmen, Indian tourists, foreigners seeking enlightenment, and tourists coming to see the whole spectacle.

Mr. Nowrojee offered me rum and hot water in an old etched glass, and I looked around his store. Everything was shoved into dusty cubbies, which were buried under piles of old newspapers and boxes of candy. We chatted for some time about the deforestation of the hills, the loss of wildlife, and the garbage problem. He used to hunt bears and leopards, until one day the Dalai Lama asked him to stop, and he did. The store was like a walk through the past, a veritable time capsule of a five-n-dime shop minus the soda fountain.

When I walked back down to Delek, I was surprised to see the hospital station wagon lying in a ditch in front of the clinic. It had slid off the icy road, and our driver was struggling to get it out of the ditch. The car was heavier than it looked, but with 10 people lifting we managed to get it back on the road. When I was pushing from behind, I glanced at the tires and saw that they were totally bald – they had no tread at all. I asked the driver if we could get new ones. New tires, he responded, would cost the equivalent of TB medicines for six patients for one year.

New tires would therefore have to wait, as the demand for TB medicines was higher than ever. We had a few severe cases at the moment, including a 55-year-old woman who had arrived a week earlier with shortness of breath. Her X-ray showed that half of her right lung was filled with fluid. Nathalie, the doctor on duty that day, inserted a needle into the space between her lung and chest wall and pulled out 1.5 liters of the most disgusting, thick, yellow fluid you can imagine. It smelled like rotten cabbage, and the odor reached clear across the hospital. After a couple more taps of the fluid, her X-ray revealed a fluid-filled cavity within her fluid-filled lung. None of us had seen anything like it. We wanted to send her for a CT scan to get a more detailed view of her lungs to characterize the extent of disease, and look for any underlying malignancy, but she couldn't afford the $40. We put her on standard TB therapy and hoped that would do the trick. Chances were that she would do fine, so a CT scan probably would have been purely academic.

The next patient to fill us with awe was a man from a nearby settlement who arrived coughing blood. He had pulmonary TB, which was not so unusual; we saw it almost every day. What was remarkable was that he also had draining channels of pus from very large lymph nodes in his neck, and draining abscesses on his right hand. Under local anesthesia, Bryan cut open the abscesses and scooped out some nasty-looking material. An X-ray of the man's hand revealed near total destruction of his wrist bones, consistent with inflammatory bone disease (known as osteomyelitis). How to put all this together? It appeared that our patient had pulmonary TB, lymph node TB, and TB osteomyelitis all at the same time. It was an incredible manifestation of the multi-faced TB bacteria (colloquially called by doctors the "red snapper" when dyed and observed under the microscope). All evening Bryan and I just kept repeating to ourselves, "I have never seen THAT before." It had become our mantra.

We ended up chanting the mantra again the next morning, when we witnessed the arrival in Dharamsala of a 1959 vintage, slightly worn, red London double-decker bus. Two crazy Englishmen and an Australian had set off from Britain 5 months prior, determined to drive the behemoth all the way to Hong Kong. They had crossed the channel to France, gone down through central Europe, Croatia, Serbia, and Bulgaria, then had gotten stuck in a snowstorm near the 17,000-foot Mount Ararat in Turkey. After they recovered, they had continued through the Middle East and Iran, and entered India via Pakistan. They (like many other tourists) had made the drive from Delhi to Dharamsala just to see the Tibetan refugee camps. I will never forget the image of their big London bus slowly lumbering through the narrow streets in our quiet little town in the foothills of the Himalayas.

The following weekend I escaped my idyllic rural town for the smog and congestion of Delhi to attend the wedding of a friend's relative. This entailed spending 12 hours on an overnight bus through the hills of Himachal and the plains of Haryana, constantly wondering if the next curve would be my last. The harrowing ride was a small price to pay for the opportunity to escape the damp chill of Dharamsala and see a traditional Indian wedding. For me, the highlights of this traditional event included the women's folk dance party and the singing of Hindi poetry by the families' elders.

On the bus ride home, I sat next to a young monk who was returning to his home at Namgyal Monastery from the Kalachakra festival. He told me about the ceremony in halting English. I mentioned that I had read in the newspaper that the Chairman of the Communist Party in China was ill and in the hospital.

"Does this mean that there will be change in China and Tibet?" he asked with a grave face.

"I hope so," I responded.

The monk looked at me squarely with his young, anxious eyes. "I hope he passes away from this world in peace," he said, his face slowly relaxing into a grin. He laughed a short laugh, as did I. He then closed his eyes and started fingering his prayer beads. He murmured his mantras to the hum of the bus wheels, in tune so much that I couldn't tell which was which. The corners of his mouth were turned slightly upward, his smile barely perceptible in the low orange blush of the sunset.

When I returned to Delek, I was confronted with a series of cases that illustrated the lower social status of women in both societies within which I was working. First, I admitted a middle-class, middle-aged Indian woman who was carried in by her three grown sons. She couldn't walk because she had severe ulcers on both feet. The men claimed the ulcers had only been there for 1 week, but I had seen plenty of foot ulcers when I was working at a public hospital in Cambridge, and I could tell that these had been there for more than a week. The woman, who turned out to be diabetic, had obviously been neglected by her family. It surprised me that a woman who had given her husband three sons would have to endure the pain of a medical problem that was more due to disregard than anything, given the value placed on bearing boys in Indian society.

The next case was far worse. A local welfare officer brought in a 35-year-old Tibetan woman who had been beaten in the head by her husband with an iron water pipe. There was a bad cut on her upper left face, and her cheekbone had been smashed in. Of course, alcohol had been involved. The woman's 7-year-old daughter came to stay with her in the hospital, and many friends stopped by.

"What will happen to her?" I asked them.

"She'll probably stay out of the house for a while," a woman answered. "She can stay with friends, but eventually the financial pressure will force her to return to her husband."

"Nothing will happen to him?"

"Nothing."

At that point, one of the wealthiest Tibetan women in McLeod Ganj walked into the hospital, covered with bruises and coughing blood. I had seen Doma a month ago on a follow-up visit for rheumatic heart disease, atrial fibrillation, and congestive heart failure. She owned a large guesthouse and could afford appropriate medications, but had decided she didn't need them. In addition, she had taken up chewing tobacco and smoking, but none of this could account for her current condition.

"What happened?" I asked, taking her into a private exam room. It turned out that she and her husband had traveled to the Kalachakra festival, where her husband had gone on a drinking spree, beaten her up, and revealed that he had a second wife. Doma barely managed the trip back to Dharamsala, and had come straight to the hospital. I admitted her for heart failure, unsure whether she would survive. Luckily we had the essential drugs for heart failure and arrhythmia, diuretics and digitalis, and she pulled through. It would have been a huge loss to the community if she hadn't made it. Unfortunately for her and many other women, I was told by more than one Tibetan that traditional values dictated that a husband had the "right" to physically abuse his wife as if she were his property. Yet I wondered, did traditional values tolerate the fact that men could abuse their wives, or were traditional values invoked by those who were abusive, as justification for their behavior? I thought not, and explained Doma's husband's behavior as characteristic of an abusive substance abuser. Luckily I saw few other instances of domestic violence during my stay. As an outsider, however, it was hard for me to delve into this issue any deeper, and despite spending nearly a year with the community my insights into women's rights were limited. From what I could tell, women had a great deal of say in everyday cultural life.

This was not unusual, as Tibetan culture at times was historically matriarchal with women having real economic power and a strong influence in community affairs. There are still several small tribes in Yunnan that are culturally related to Tibet where women play an important role in society. The Mosuo in Yunnan are a unique minority that still practice Tibetan Buddhism, and are one of the few Chinese minorities that continue to have a true matriarchal culture with women holding power. The Naxi, another minority in Yunnan whose people are descendant from Tibetan nomads, is a matrilineal culture where property and political power are passed down through generations from mother to daughter. Political power, however, is still held by men. Matrilineal is, of course, not the same as matriarchal. What I often wondered about in this refugee community was whether Tibetans retained any remnant of that matriarchal tradition, or was that something that had changed just like many other things had?

It's appealing to imagine that cultures don't change. I had often heard foreigners voice an opinion that Tibetan society was a "pure culture" without the faults of corrupt, materialistic Western societies. This ideal has been perpetuated in Western literature and film, from James Hilton's image of Shangri-la from his 1933 novel Lost Horizon, to contemporary stories of the French comic book hero Tintin and his adventures in Tibet. The concept of domestic violence within the Tibetan community seemed impossible to these idealists. The truth was that the Tibetan refugee community was like any other – the pressures of leaving home and of having no job, no education, and poor prospects drove some men to alcohol and violence. The women ended up bearing the brunt of all the poverty and social disarray. I felt that fixing these community issues, however, was out of my control.

The situation was depressing, and I was grateful for the occasional comfort of correspondence from home. While some of my friends wrote about politics or movies or current events, my favorite letters were those from my maternal grandmother, who wrote about the farm in western Iowa and the winter storms that swept across the plains. Although I had been nurtured by my parents in an urban environment, I have to admit that sometimes news of my grandmother's farm was comforting and just what I wanted to hear.

The other welcome distraction during winter at Delek Hospital was getting a roll of film developed. Our social schedule was so limited that the hospital volunteers organized entire dinners or parties around the anticipation of seeing new pictures. It sounds a bit desperate, but we had to find ways to break the routine and stay cheerful.

After my first 6 months in Dharamsala, I realized that I had lost 18 pounds. I was down to 160 pounds (11 1/2 stone, according to my English colleagues) – about right for my height of 5'9", except now all my pants were too large, my shirts were too loose, and my belts lacked small enough holes. There was only one solution – take a vacation. As it happened, my 1-year visa prohibited me from staying in India longer than 6 months at a time, so I had to leave the country and reenter. I decided to spend a couple of weeks in Thailand, basking on the beach and eating as much coconut-milk curry and chocolate as I liked.

9

A Trip to Chandigarh

My first week back from winter vacation turned out to be dizzying. The first day began badly, when a young woman in her third trimester came in with a complaint that you never want to hear – she said she could no longer feel her baby moving. We sent her to Zonal Hospital for an ultrasound, hoping for the best. Sadly for all, she came back with a report stating that there was no detectable heart rhythm or fetal movement. I referred her to the nearest secondary care hospital (an hour and a half away) for an urgent cesarean section, hoping that she wouldn't go into septic shock on the way. Of course, we never heard back about the referral. I couldn't stop thinking about how sad it must be to carry to near term only to have a stillborn child.

The next patient was a woman in her eighth week of pregnancy who reported passing large clots of blood. I whisked her upstairs to our inpatient ward for Michael to evaluate her for a miscarriage, wondering if my entire day was going to be like this. It turned out to be much worse.

Four days earlier, Bryan had admitted a woman who had experienced a gradual onset of headaches, fever, and loss of appetite. By the time she was brought to Delek Hospital, she was practically delirious and had a severely stiff neck. As she was being admitted, she had three grand mal seizures. Bryan did a lumbar puncture, which showed cloudy fluid, and put her on penicillin and chloramphenicol (an antibiotic that kills a broad array of bacteria) for a presumptive diagnosis of meningitis. The microbiology color stains of her cerebral spinal fluid were negative, though Bryan was sure she had meningitis. Over the next 3 days she had remained much the same, with waxing and waning levels of consciousness, until her fever and stiff neck abated. Then she suddenly developed specific

neurologic signs, including deviation of her eyes to the left, a motion-
less and paralyzed left side, and a declining mental status. Michael,
who was on call for the week, wanted to send her to the tertiary care
hospital in Chandigarh for a CT scan. He was worried about a mass
lesion in her brain. As I was off that day, I volunteered to make the 6-
hour trip with the patient and her family. My days off always ended
up being on call if I hung around the hospital.

The woman's husband, a waiter at the Hotel Lhasa, secured a
minivan taxi from his neighbor. We set off at noon, winding our way
through Himachal Pradesh toward the plains of the Punjab. Our taxi
driver was a man of about 25 who spoke broken English at best.
About half an hour into the drive, he stopped at a gas station, casu-
ally got out, and announced that he wanted to change the tires. Meanwhile, the patient was cramped in the back seat, barely conscious,
moaning, and breathing heavily. I implored the driver to hurry, but he
seemed to brush me off as another anxious foreigner. After fifteen
minutes and a bowl of rice for each of us, we set off again.

As we reached the southern part of Himachal, it quickly became
apparent that our driver did not know his way to Chandigarh. This
surprised me, given that it is one of the largest cities in northern
India. He stopped at nearly every intersection, asking directions from
anybody he could find. First it was another taxi driver, then a rick-
shaw puller, then a farmer. It took us 5 hours just to reach Una, the
nearest medium-sized town. We still had at least another 2 hours to
go, and the sun had already begun to set. I started to feel like I was in
a bad horror movie. Luckily, the patient's condition did not seem to
be deteriorating, so I kept my head buried in a copy of *The Nation*
that a friend had sent me in the mail. I can't explain why, but reading
political commentary soothed my nerves.

We finally reached Chandigarh at 7 p.m. after an excruciating
number of stops for directions. The next problem was maneuvering
our way through the city's confusing layout. Chandigarh, which dou-
bles as the capital of both the Punjab and Haryana states, was
planned by the Swiss/French architect Le Corbusier between 1950
and 1965. It is also known as the "city of roses," although I saw none
during my short stay. The entire city was built on a grid system, with

roundabouts at every intersection. It should have been easy to navigate, except that every roundabout looked the same at twilight. There weren't many buildings or landmarks, so it felt like we were still driving through the countryside, going around in endless circles. I had lost all sense of direction, and the driver obviously had no idea where he was going, so once again we had to stop at every corner to ask for directions to the Postgraduate Medical Institute. Even if someone told the driver to go through five roundabouts and turn right, he still stopped on the next block to ask someone else. If you have ever asked for directions in India, you know that if you ask five people, you'll get five very polite but very different answers. I was on the verge of losing my cool, but managed to keep it together since the patient was still stable.

When we finally got to the Postgraduate Medical Institute at about 8 p.m., I ran into the building, only to find myself lost in the huge corridors. I eventually made it to the medical emergency ward. As I scanned the raucous crowd of patients and their families, I realized "emergency care" did not translate to "immediate care." There must have been two dozen patients lying in stretchers, scattered like sheep on a hill, moaning, groaning, vomiting, wailing, and crying while cockroaches climbed the walls. To add to the mayhem, a dog ran through the room. There were only two doctors working in a flurry to handle all the patients, while two nurses sat behind a desk and did paperwork. It was a scene I'll never forget, one of runaway pandemonium.

I resigned myself to the fact that they would get to my patient when they got to her, and I tried to reassure her husband. As I stood against the wall, waiting, I spied a slightly older Indian lecturing a younger doctor over the convulsing body of a frail 10-year-old girl. Seeing an "in," I walked over and asked the nature of the patient's condition. The doctors probably saw few foreigners in their dilapidated institution, and they took an interest in me immediately.

"Organophosphate pesticide poisoning," the older doctor told me, referring to the little girl.

"I would never have thought of that," I replied, adding that I was a physician volunteering in Dharamsala.

He stared at me amiably, yet in disbelief. "I can't imagine why any American in his right mind would come to work in India. You could be in the U.S. making ends meet and more."

"I like what I'm doing here," I said simply. I went on to tell him about my background, and it turned out that he had one brother working as a doctor at the Deaconess Hospital in Boston and another at the National Institutes of Health in Washington. I surmised correctly that he was a neurologist and finally asked him to see my patient.

After taking a history from the husband, he did a brief but thorough exam, and I could tell he was an experienced and talented clinician. When he asked me what I thought, I hesitated. According to the husband, the woman started having headaches about a month before her seizures began. The scenario sounded familiar.

"Could be TB meningitis," I said finally, thinking of Tenzin. "We had a monk with that diagnosis at Delek Hospital several months ago."

The neurologist agreed and asked his resident to do a CT scan and repeat lumbar puncture. It was exactly what I had hoped for. After thanking the doctor for his kindness and reassuring the patient's husband that she was in good care despite the apparent purgatorial surroundings, I went outside to breathe some fresh air.

When I came across a food stall, I realized I hadn't had anything substantial to eat since breakfast. The stall, in typical eclectic Indian English, offered, "Fresh Frut Juce and Tomato Soop – free of any added colour or flovour." At least they spelled "tomato" correctly (which was better than former U.S. Vice President Dan Quayle, who was well known for his misspellings, had done with "potato(e)"). I laughed and ordered some "soop" which had a delicious natural "flovour."

An hour later, the confused taxi driver finally returned to pick me up outside the hospital. I asked him to drive me back to Dharamsala, which he excitedly declined to do.

"We'll stay here for the night," he said. "I'll stay with my sister. You can stay at a hotel."

If his sister lived in Chandigarh, I wondered, why hadn't he known the way? His brother-in-law leaned out of the minivan just then and asked me in broken English which hotel I wanted to stay at for the night.

"I absolutely have to get back to Dharamsala," I insisted. "I'm scheduled for clinic duty in the morning." At this point, both men pretended not to understand me. I climbed into the back seat, not sure what else to do.

"Which hotel?" the brother-in-law asked again.

"Look, I only have $5 with me," I replied. They laughed at the sight of a foreigner with so little cash. Then we began driving around an endless series of roundabouts, stopping at hotels to check for vacancies. For some reason, they were all full.

It was nearing 10 p.m., and the prospect of driving 7 hours in the dark sounded less and less appealing and more and more dangerous. As we continued roaming around Chandigarh, the driver and his brother-in-law were obviously talking about me, but I had no idea what they were saying. I felt like a corpse that two murderers were trying to figure out where to dump.

We eventually pulled into Punjab University, and the brother-in-law brought me through some alleys into a giant dining hall. By this time everyone was done eating, but there were handfuls of students drinking tea and chatting, while Hindi music blared over the sputtering speakers. It turned out that the brother-in-law was a dishwasher there, so he figured it would be a reasonable place to dispose of me for the night.

Dinner consisted of Ramen noodles and a Coke, and conversations with the students about how I landed in their cafeteria in the middle of a Monday night. They all thought it was an incredible story. After 6 months in India, nothing was beyond my credulity in this country. But I thought I'd never see Delek Hospital again.

A 22-year-old chemistry student named Sundeep suggested I spend the night in his dorm room, which ended up being a good enough solution. I never asked why the brother-in-law didn't let me sleep on the floor of his own home. Indians are usually the most hospitable people on earth, so I figured there must have been something embarrassing at home. It was possible that he felt his dwelling was too poor to accommodate a foreigner.

Before the driver and his brother-in-law could take off, I asked Sundeep to explain that we absolutely had to leave for Dharamsala before 6 a.m. The men nodded and took their leave, just as the Punjabi sky broke open and dumped buckets of rain into the alleys. I was glad not to be making the arduous drive home on dark, wet roads.

Sundeep led me down the long, dim corridors of Boys Hostel Number 3. He took me into a cement room that would have been drab, but for the posters of Indian and American actresses plastered on the walls, most of whom I didn't recognize. I suddenly felt old, the Farah Fawcett posters of my childhood replaced by younger, more nubile models. My guest offered me tea, and we chatted about school and gender relations. Sundeep told me about a woman he secretly wanted to date, but was not able to, given the strict social mores of his parents and peers. If a man and woman were seen together, it was assumed they would eventually get married. Women and men weren't allowed to hold hands, let alone touch each other in public. His parents were trying to pressure him into an arranged marriage which he had so far refused. His frustrations left me with the impression that India was a very sexually repressed society. After several hours of discussion, I finally collapsed on a box spring with a thin mattress and one blanket. I had left Delek in such a hurry that morning, I hadn't even packed my toothbrush.

I woke up at 5 a.m. Of course, the taxi driver didn't turn up until 7:30 a.m. I was irritated, but realized that someone would do my clinic for me anyway, and I should just relax and try to enjoy the ride. This proved difficult, as it became clear that the trip was going to be a replay in reverse of the previous day's journey. The driver was out of his territory and once again had no idea where he was going. It took nearly an hour just to get out of Chandigarh. Several times on the way to Nangal, then Una, I was the one who recognized the intersections and implored him to make the proper turns.

Around 10 a.m. we had to stop because one of the tires was smoking. The driver changed it in 5 minutes, one of the only things he seemed to be good at doing. An hour later, the sky opened up again with rain and pebble-sized hail. We charged ahead at the minivan's top speed, and I was sure we would hydroplane right off the road into the green Punjabi fields.

"Slow down!" I yelled, realizing how silly I sounded after insisting that we get back to Delek as quickly as possible. The driver looked thoroughly confused. I put my head down and read.

When I looked up, the surroundings were unfamiliar. We weren't going back the same way we had come the day before.

"Could we stop for lunch?" I asked, planning to check directions on my own. "I didn't have any breakfast."

"Five minutes, five minutes," he said.

I read some more. The road became a river of mud. I asked to stop again and got the same answer. By 1 p.m., I was through with my Bertrand Russell essay, *Mysticism and Logic,* and very, very hungry.

"We have to stop," I insisted.

"Five minutes, five minutes," came the driver's new mantra.

Thirty minutes later, we reached a small town called Nurpur. He jumped out, hugged several men, and told me to sit down in his brother's food shop. It dawned on me that we were in his hometown. I had been so stupid, but there was nothing I could do. I ate food enough for two and for some unknown reason, ended up paying for his lunch as well. Then I waited under a leaky roof while the rain fell, and he recounted his version of the events to his friends and brothers.

When he finished socializing, he had the nerve to ask me for money to buy gas. "We won't make it all the way back otherwise," he said ominously.

How had I gotten myself into this situation? I was stuck with a recalcitrant, petulant taxi driver who had taken me to his out-of-the-way hometown against my will, and now wanted me to pay for the extra gas. I had no choice but to give him the last of my cash.

We climbed back into the taxi, he cranked up the Hindi movie tunes, and we were off. Himachal was his turf, so he drove like a bat out of hell. When we hit a main road around 2:30 in the afternoon, I realized where we were: on the road to Pathankot, west of Dharamsala; Chandigarh was straight south. He had gone completely out of his way to visit his town, and we were still an hour and a half from Dharamsala. It was like driving through Wyoming on the way from Denver, Colorado, to Lincoln, Nebraska. It was practically in the other direction.

"Why did we come this way?" I asked loudly, beginning to lose my temper.

"The road was safer," he answered. Considering that we had been speeding along on a wet road with bald tires, I doubted safety was his top concern. Clearly, he had no feelings of responsibility toward getting me back to work on time, let alone the safety of the patient the day before.

We finally reached Delek Hospital in the late afternoon, after 8 hours on the road. It was beyond my comprehension why the patient's family had decided not to take the hospital car. Our driver would have made the same trip in 5 or 6 hours each way. Now I had lost a day at work, been cheated out of gas money, and felt like a ball of dirt. To top it off, I had Hindi movie music stuck in my head.

There was nothing I wanted more than a hot shower, so of course, the power went out and rendered my coil immersion heater useless. As I collapsed on the bed in my near-freezing room, my only hope was that the patient would survive. Otherwise the whole nightmarish trip would have been in vain. I had survived the frustration of the long trip, but I was less certain that my patient would. I would not find out the outcome for several weeks.

The Perils of Celebration

The Tibetan New Year, known as Losar, didn't come until the beginning of March, but preparations for the festivities began weeks ahead of time. Houses received fresh coats of blue and white paint, women bought newly made traditional Tibetan aprons, and men got new haircuts. In the days following my trip to Chandigarh, the holiday was all the hospital staff talked about: whose friends and family were coming to visit, what types of food would be served, how much *chang* (rice wine) everyone would drink.

Two evenings before Losar, the more traditional families made big dumplings with special symbols inside, such as a piece of coal or a coin. At dinner, each person received a dumpling predicting his or her karma for the year. Coal suggested a bad temper, while a coin meant the recipient would be getting plenty of money.

The day before Losar began, the hospital experienced a sudden epidemic of health – apparently many of our inpatients wanted to be home for the holiday. After an entire day spent discharging patients, one of the nurses predicted that the ward wouldn't stay quiet for long. "Lots of injuries and illnesses occur during Losar," she warned. As if on cue, a man who had eaten bad pork came in and began vomiting violently on our floor. I realized I was in for a rough time, being the only doctor on duty for the entire four and a half days of celebrations.

On Losar Eve, the monks at the Dalai Lama's monastery threw out all the bad spirits from the previous year. Then precisely at midnight, some of the old village stalwarts rushed out to look for the first fresh spring water of the year. By 4 a.m., the festivities were in full swing. I awoke to the sound of firecrackers and the rumble of taxis taking people up the mountain road to the main temple. There were roving groups of Tibetans, who probably had had a little too much to drink, walking around yelling *"Tashi delek!"* for everyone to hear. Losar was obviously the biggest celebration of the year.

At 8 a.m., I was able to leave the hospital for a few hours to watch the official New Year's Day ceremony. The main temple was packed full of revelers, but I had a great view of ornately dressed Tibetan monks in tall yellow hats, playing the long brass horns that are reserved for special occasions. Hundreds of Tibetans chanted, and the Dalai Lama sat on his platform seat, praying. According to the Tibetan calendar, in which each year corresponds to one of 12 animals and one of five elements, we were bidding goodbye to the Wood-Dog Year and hello to the Wood-Pig Year.

Ministers from the government brought in offerings, mainly sculptures made of butter known as *tormas* in large bowls, huge home-made crackers called *kabsay*, and plenty of white scarves. I was later told that each *torma* has a specific characteristic according to the deity to whom it is offered. All *tormas* have three fundamental elements, foundation, body, and decoration, that symbolize the qualities of body, speech, and mind. As the offerings continued, several monks debated in humorous fashion, while others scurried among the observers to hand out tea and small plates of freshly prepared rice, the first of the year. After the prayers, everyone was given a blessed red cord to be worn around the neck for protection against evil spirits. The Dalai Lama then walked onto a balcony overlooking the crowd and gave a short speech. His Holiness is known for his humor even while giving serious teachings, and he didn't disappoint today. He told the crowd that he knew everyone was going to drink *chang*, but being the father figure he was, he told them just to not overdo it!

When I ran back to the hospital, I found some patients who would have benefited from hearing their spiritual leader's speech and following his advice. One of the waiters at the Hotel Tibet had fallen down a full flight of stairs, cutting the top of his head wide open. The blood was all over our emergency room and still flowing from his cut. Despite the early hour, he was quite drunk, as were the other waiters who brought him in.

While I sewed up the jagged laceration, I asked one of the other waiters to put pressure on the wound to stop the blood flow. Although the patient was thrashing around on the bed, I managed to clean the cut and put in 10 sutures. Then I looked up and saw that my helper was the husband of the woman we had transferred to Chandigarh 2 weeks ago.

"How is your wife?" I asked.

The man looked away. "They found a brain tumor. She died 3 days later."

A brain tumor? I didn't believe it. There had been pus in her cerebral spinal fluid, suggesting meningitis. Either she had a secondary infection, or the brain tumor diagnosis was wrong. We would likely never know. In any case, I was quite sad to learn that she had died. My disappointment, however, was nothing compared to the husband's sorrow. He was so distraught that he had apparently taken up the bottle to relieve his pain.

"I don't want to lose my friend," he cried in his inebriated state. "Please doctor, I just lost my wife. I have nothing to live for."

I was moved by his sorrow. "Your friend is not going to die," I assured him. I finished patching the patient up and recommended a CT scan to be sure he hadn't sustained a subdural hematoma. Watching all the waiters bundle into a taxi, I hoped that the driver hadn't been drinking as well.

I expected the rest of the day would be calm by comparison, but I was wrong. I was sitting at the nurses' station, which had a clear view of the hospital's driveway, when an Indian white Ambassador taxi pulled up. Three men tumbled out, ran in, and talked excitedly to our nurse Youdon for several minutes. Moments later I got a succinct, one-sentence synopsis.

"There's a man in there that had an accident," Youdon told me, pointing to the Ambassador.

"OK, what kind of accident?" I asked impatiently.

"He fell off a train."

I had to pry her for details.

"I see. How did he fall off a train?"

"Actually, he jumped out," she clarified.

I looked at the patient's friends. "Why did he do that?"

Youdon spoke with the men for a minute, then translated. "They were all sleeping in the train car when he suddenly started yelling about his ancestors and spirits, ran to the door of the train, and jumped."

"Wow," I said, quite surprised. It was an amazing story so far. "Where did this happen?"

"In Maharashtra."

"What?"

I quickly tried to do the math. Maharashtra was the western Indian state containing Mumbai (Bombay), on the Indian Ocean coastline.

"That's got to be over 1,500 miles away!"

Youdon stared at me with a classic Tibetan look that I had learned to appreciate for its dark irony. Her face was blank, providing no clue as to what she thought about the situation. For all I knew she was as shocked as I was, but from her appearance it seemed like a routine call.

"How in the world did his friends find him?" I was ready for any answer.

"They pulled the cord and jumped out after him as the train slowed down."

"When did this happen?" I asked, afraid to hear the answer.

"Three days ago."

"Three days ago?" I repeated, disbelievingly. "Has he seen a doctor yet?"

"Yes, well, they drove to Delhi, and the health worker in the Tibetan refugee camp referred them up here."

"Are you trying to tell me that these fellows drove for two and a half days half way across India with an injured friend in the back seat to come see us at Delek Hospital?"

"Yes that is what I'm telling you."

We all paused.

By this time, I was totally incredulous. For a resident of the U.S., it was nearly equivalent to someone jumping off a train as it neared Chicago, getting in a taxi and driving to Washington, D.C., seeing a nurse, and getting referred to Boston for medical care. The story was completely and utterly crazy, but I had gotten used to these kinds of surprises.

I had them bring in the patient, who was a middle-aged Tibetan from one of the southern settlements. He was covered with bruises and scratches and did indeed look like he had jumped out of a speeding train, although I have to admit that I had never before actually seen anyone who had jumped out of a speeding train. I guessed he was an alcoholic. He had probably tried to quit cold turkey, experienced withdrawal hallucinations, and really did think he saw his ancestors' spirits. After examining him and doing a plethora of X-rays, all I found was a small fracture in his ankle and a cut on his lip. Amazing. I couldn't help but say it again – "I've never seen that before."

I figured I had a lock on the most unusual case of the year, until I shared the story with Michael that evening. He listened with a grin before bursting my bubble. "Oh yeah?! The other day, I saw someone who jumped off a train in the South and drove up to Himachal Pradesh for an X-ray."

I couldn't believe he had bested my story.

"Do you think this kind of thing is common?" I asked him. "Maybe Tibetans would rather drive thousands of miles to go to a Tibetan facility than visit Indian hospitals – even though the Indian facilities are at least as good."

Michael didn't have time to answer, because just then a group of Tibetans walked in carrying an old woman who had fallen on the *lingkor* path. An X-ray revealed she had fractured her right thigh bone in three places. The poor woman had traveled thousands of miles–from Tibet to India by foot, then to Dharamsala by bus–only to fall while doing her religious circumambulations around the Dalai Lama's residence. I wanted to send her to Chandigarh, but the family had no money. An orthopedic surgeon visiting from New York suggested putting in a Steinmann pin and rigging up traction on her leg for a couple of weeks. Unfortunately, Dr. Tsetan said that the hospital had no Steinmann pin. We wanted to check for one in the orthopedic procedure sterile pack, but it was locked, and the head nurse was at home celebrating Losar. So I reluctantly sent the old woman to the local hospital, where she was probably treated with bed rest. Later, I learned that there was a Steinmann pin in the orthopedic pack. Poor inventory lists of our equipment, along with the policy of keeping equipment locked up, meant we had missed the opportunity to help a patient.

I got little response when I discussed this incident with the doctor-in-charge. Tibetans in general did not admit mistakes, perhaps out of a fear of being reprimanded. I had never heard one say, "I'm sorry," even if someone caused harm to another or failed to carry out an important task. I had seen full-grown adults make up all kinds of excuses, even "white lies," to cover up the slightest wrongdoing or forgetfulness. In my experience, this compulsion to "save face" was standard practice throughout Asia.

On the positive side, what some Tibetans lacked in candor, they made up for in hospitality. On the second day of Losar, several families invited me over for tea, then lunch, and then *chang*. Unfortunately, I only had time to escape the hospital once and chose to visit a young couple in McLeod Ganj. Namgyal, the wife, spoke excellent English and held a bachelor's degree in political science from Delhi University. Yet, she was at home cooking and taking care of her husband's parents, as cultural expectations dictated. Though I had rarely seen Tibetans show emotion in their facial expressions or tone of voice, I could sense Namgyal's frustration. Of course, I knew better than to ask her how she felt about the situation. I had found Tibetans to be very introverted people, never revealing their feelings to strangers and probably not even to friends and family.

Ironically, Tibetans did seem to enjoy talking about other people's feelings. An anthropology student I met told me the residents of Dharamsala thrived on gossip. Single women especially were targets. Being seen with a man was tantamount to having an illicit affair to some. The problem was so severe that single female friends of mine refused to be seen walking down the street with me. They were too concerned the gossip mill would start grinding out news that they were seen with the foreign doctor and something must be going on.

On the last day of Losar, I took a break from ward duty to watch the Dalai Lama leave his residence and drive by on his way to another settlement. As his car slowed on the big hairpin turn near the hospital, he looked out the window of his yellow Mercedes, smiled at me, and said, *"Tashi delek."* I wondered whether he had even imagined the perils of being a doctor on call during Losar. By the time holiday was over, the tally for my stint on call included four persons with fractures, three cases of food poisoning, a couple of people with psychotic episodes, and a number of drunks who had fallen down and gotten banged up.

The week following Losar was full of surprises. First, an American studying Buddhism in Dharamsala began teaching yoga classes on the hospital's roof. Dharamsala attracted many types of foreigners, itinerant backpack travelers, bona fide tourists, and those who genuinely wanted to start a new life in a peaceful place. In a sense they were all seeking a peaceful resting place, as were the Tibetans, but some stayed longer than others. I liked our yoga teacher, but I knew that her stay here would be limited like mine, that some day she would move on again, seeking another place to call home, if even for a short time. As for myself and yoga, I tried a few of the positions, but I must admit I like tai ch'i better.

The next surprise was the opportunity to hear a Tibetan rock band practice in a nearby mountain village. The Dalai Lama had named the group, which had just cut its first album, the "The Yak Band." As far as I knew, it was the only Tibetan rock band on the planet. The Yak Band performed original songs in Tibetan, as well as covering some Western tunes in English and Hindi. The lead guitarist did a pretty good Eric Clapton impression. After the practice, he and his wife invited me to dinner. They served roast chicken that surpassed anything I had eaten all year. How they did it without an oven, I'll never know.

When I returned to Delek Hospital, a German hairdresser had arrived with homemade carrot cake and chocolate cake. She gave all of the volunteers haircuts for $2 each. Anything new or unusual was an excuse for a celebration, so we made a haircutting party with tea and cake. She did an excellent job rescuing me from my previous haircut, which looked like the barber had put a bowl over my head and shaved around it.

Clinic the next morning brought more surprises, beginning with a monk who came in complaining of a severely swollen right knee. He had traveled from Tibet to southern India for the Kalachakra festival, carrying all of his belongings over the Himalayas. At the ceremony, he apparently was so moved by the sight of the Dalai Lama that he spent most of the 7 days prostrating himself on the ground, standing up, praying, then prostrating again. Only afterward did he begin to feel the pain in his knee. His problem was neither arthritis nor a joint effusion, but bursitis of his kneecap, colloquially known in medicine by its eponym, "nursemaid's knee." It's a common problem among people who spend a lot of time on their knees, such as carpet layers, wrestlers, and floor cleaners. We drained the fluid from his kneecap and put him on antibiotics, renaming the condition "Tibetan prostrator's knee" in his honor.

Then a woman named Dechen, who had delivered her first child a few weeks earlier, showed up asking for a postnatal exam and well-baby check. While this kind of thing is routine in the U.S., and rightly so, I just looked at her as if she were from Mars. No one in Dharamsala had ever come in asking me for a preventive health check before. I was stunned and then realized she was perfectly right. Later I reflected on how the contextual demands of my environment had impacted my praxis (practice). I had completely changed from a "preventive" outlook of practice – preventive medicine had made up half of my medical work in Cambridge – to a "treat as many illnesses as you can" approach in a developing world setting. Such change can creep up on you without making a sound, and before you know it, you're no longer practicing in the way you intended.

Just when I thought we were experiencing a reprieve, TB struck back in disguise. Another monk came in that afternoon, complaining that his throat had been sore for the past 3 weeks, and that his feet were swollen. The weather was still so cold that he was wearing a down jacket, even inside the clinic. When I asked him to take off the jacket, the real problem became clear: a belly full of ascites fluid and large, matted lymph nodes all up and down his neck. His X-ray showed a chest full of TB as well.

Despite our best efforts to treat him, the monk deteriorated rapidly over the following week. He developed a partial small bowel obstruction, could not eat, and began losing weight. Dark brown fecal-like material dripped out of his newly placed nasal-gastric tube, and his abdomen bloated up with gas. I suspected a fistula between his stomach and his bowel, but couldn't be sure whether his TB was to blame for it. All I could do was give him fluids and try to decompress his bowels. He refused to see a surgeon and died 10 days after he arrived. Monks from the nearby monastery spent the night chanting songs from the Tibetan Book of the Dead, a haunting sound I had become used to in our small mountain village.

Watching patients die was the hardest aspect of my work at Delek Hospital. It was especially frustrating when a patient refused treatment, as was the case with a 70-year-old man from the Elders Home. Tsetan Karma was well known among older Tibetans for being a former freedom fighter for Tibetan independence. The guerrilla army called Chushi Gangdrug had been crushed in the early 1970s by the Nepalese. The Chinese had apparently grown tired of the last remaining fighters in the remote areas of the Himalayas and had pushed Nepal to crush the Tibetan resistance once and for all. Through blackmail, starvation, and ruthless forays into the mountains, the Nepalese managed to capture or kill nearly all of the force. I didn't know how Tsetan Karma came to live in Dharamsala, but it was obvious that he had once been a formidable man, well built, strong, and forceful. Now he was crumpled up in a little ball on his bed in Delek Hospital.

The disease that had reduced him to this state was atherosclerosis, or hardening of the arteries. The blood supply to his feet had become so scant that his toes and feet were turning black from lack of oxygen. He was obviously in pain, though he was too proud to admit it. The only treatment would have been amputation, which he refused. And so he sat in his bed with black, disfigured feet, in obvious pain most of the time, but always denying that he was uncomfortable.

It was very hard to watch this process, knowing that I could have relieved his suffering. As an ethical physician, however, I could not force a treatment on a patient without consent. I told him that it wouldn't be long before his feet became gangrenous. "The rotten tissue will get infected," I explained, "and you will die." Still, he refused any help. I concluded that he had made up his mind to die. Perhaps the saddest part was that he was completely alone during this time. This fact had physical ramifications as well as the obvious psychological strain. Nurses in India generally did not feed and wash patients; family members or friends were expected to stop by and help with food and hygiene. Tsetan Karma had no family and no friends his age, so he was stuck in bed unable to eat or care for himself. The volunteer physicians helped him sometimes, but we couldn't stay by his side all day. I was surprised that no one from the old guerrilla army came to help. Perhaps they were all gone. I wondered whether the Dalai Lama's path of nonviolence discouraged the recognition of former freedom fighters. Ex-guerilla or not, I wondered what other resources the refugee community might have mustered for an elder Tibetan on his deathbed.

In addition to patients who refused treatment, we occasionally had to deal with people intent on self-destruction. Doma, the wealthy guesthouse owner with congestive heart failure, had returned to the hospital smelling like cigarettes. She had survived the previous month's beating by her unfaithful husband, but had not been taking her medications. This, combined with her nicotine habit, was taking a toll on her heart. Now we discovered she was addicted to the tranquilizer diazepam as well. She tried to hide the pills when Michael looked in her pocket. I felt very sorry for her, but there was little we could do. Delek Hospital obviously had no addiction recovery program.

Doma's behavior reminded me of a talk on "good motivation" given by the Dalai Lama's youngest brother. Tenzin Choegyal was the spitting image of his brother, even sharing the same manner of speech and sense of humor, though his English was much better. He had been recognized at a young age as a reincarnated lama and was given the name Ngari Rinpoche. Ngari was the name of an area in Ladakh over which he served as the religious head. When he was in his teens, however, he disrobed, went to university, and later decided to get married. For many years, he worked in the Dalai Lama's private office, but he became so incapacitated by stress that he retired at the age of 45. Now he was running a famous, celebrity-friendly guesthouse in the woods near Delek Hospital, called Kashmir Cottage. Ngari Rinpoche still performed his religious duties in Ladakh, but he admitted that he didn't like doing it. We dubbed him the "Reluctant Rinpoche."

While conducting our grand rounds (conference) at the hospital one week, Ngari Rinpoche explained that Buddhists have a responsibility to pursue good motivation, while liberating themselves from hatred and ignorance. "It is of paramount importance that one's motivation is well-placed," he said, "for it affects every aspect in your life and the lives of others. Each individual will have different avenues of motivation, but all must converge on good intention. *Samsara,* or the cycle of suffering, which ultimately gives rise to poor motivation, is the bond from which all beings must free themselves."

While Doma's self-destructive behavior was understandable considering the suffering caused by her husband, it was her duty as a Buddhist to overcome this cycle. How could she achieve this? According to Ngari Rinpoche, the tools for success included patience, mindfulness, generosity, wisdom, and perseverance. To strictly follow Buddhist teachings, she had to let go of her immediate suffering and other aspects of her life on earth that were causing her harm. Her more immediate source of motivation was to break the cycle of harm she was subjected to now. What was more proper as a good Buddhist was to take the longer view, of motivation for lasting happiness and contentment. One example of true motivation would be to help her husband break his cycle of suffering.

I found the talk interesting, but unfulfilling in some respects. Ngari Rinpoche gave very few specifics about what one's motivation should be other than "helping others" and "being good." In addition, I felt good motivation was not a guarantee of good outcomes. For example, Indian midwives surely had the best intentions when they put cow dung on the umbilical stumps of newborns to promote healing. The problem was not bad motivation, but bad information – they were unaware of the existence of germs such as tetanus and anthrax.

While my motivation for working at Delek Hospital certainly fit into the category of "helping others," plenty of my actions on a daily basis had more selfish motives. While on call one afternoon, I skipped out to attend yet another wedding, my motivation being the simple desire to have a good time with friends. The bride and groom were Scottish dentists who had worked at Delek and decided to have an Indian wedding at the Shiva temple nearby. When I walked in, the *baba sadhu* with his long white beard was playing drums, singing, and taking big puffs on his marijuana pipe. The pipe went around the room, which was filled mostly with Indians. Being on call, however, I declined to join in.

After a while, the *sadhu* remembered why we were all there, fumbled around in the corner, and pulled out a book. He blew off the dust, slapped the cover a few times, and began reading. I surmised that he hadn't married anyone for a few years. Despite a fire in the center of the room, the tiny temple was so dark that I could barely make out his form, which made the whole proceeding that much more mystical. Finally, the bride came in the side door decked out in a gilded sari, her hands painted with henna in the traditional manner. She was accompanied by two dozen Indian women dressed in their wedding finest. The bride and groom sat down in front of the *sadhu*, and he sang some more songs. He ultimately joined their hands together and said several prayers. The bride had tears streaming down her face, though not from being overcome by the emotion of the event. The room was so full of ganja and fire smoke that all of our eyes were stinging and tearing. My eyes burned so badly, I had to sneak out early through the back door.

When I returned to the hospital, a message was waiting for me. More than 2 months after I had written the Information Department about the child labor problem, I had finally received a response. The Secretary of Information and Foreign Relations wanted to meet with me to discuss my concerns.

I thought about some of the Bihari children I had met in Dharamsala. One young waiter was so charming, I could have sworn he was taking lessons from a hidden stash of Cary Grant movies. When I told him he looked nice in his new clothes one evening, he replied, "I know… but didn't I look good yesterday?" His confidence masked the fact that he had been taken away from his true home and family, and was not being given access to an education.

A young Indian woman who worked in the same restaurant told me she had been there so long that she had no idea where her real home was. She worked from 7 a.m. to 10 p.m. 7 days a week, with only 3 days off per year. In exchange, she received food, shelter, and a monthly salary equal to what most laborers made in 4 days. I didn't ask her if she had been sexually abused, since we had just met. For the sake of children like her, I hoped my letter had been taken seriously.

When I arrived at the secretary's office the next day, he greeted me warmly. "Thank you for your letter. I was traveling and did not have the time to respond earlier."

"Thank you very much for meeting with me," I replied. "I know this is a touchy subject."

"As I'm sure you realize, the problem is not unique to Dharamsala, but occurs throughout India."

"Yes, and it is illegal throughout India," I pointed out. I hoped I wasn't about to hear the "everyone is doing it" excuse.

"I shared your letter with the other government ministers. We decided to send a letter of our own to each of the settlements reminding all Tibetans that child labor is a violation of the law."

My pulse quickened. Had I heard correctly? Had my letter actually sparked some sort of action?

"Will reminding the settlers of the law make any difference?" I asked.

"The problem is that there has been no enforcement. It's important to make sure our people know the Tibetan government's position. Our letter urges those who employ children to stop doing so. In addition, we want to make sure those children already taken from Bihar receive a proper education."

I left the office on a high. I knew it wouldn't have worked if just any foreigner had written such a letter. Because of my work at Delek Hospital, the government ministers regarded me as a friend of Tibet and appreciated my candor. Now the issue of child labor was on their agenda.

11

Springtime Stories of Torture and Hardship

One unusually warm morning near the end of winter, 40 sick people showed up in our morning outpatient clinic. I couldn't manage by myself and had to call Michael down to help. I was thankful for the other physicians volunteering here with me, as we all generally pitched in to help each other out in times of need. All I remember is a blur of patients with colds and the flu. That was when I realized how dependent the community was on the clinic – people came to see us just to ask for common medicine for a cough or a headache. In developed countries we are used to going to the local pharmacy to buy cough syrup and medicine for our flu symptoms, as well as over-the-counter medications that used to require a prescription, like stomach acid blockers. But here, due to poverty and lack of access to public health information, the community completely relied on the clinic and its doctors. Ultimately, Delek Hospital would benefit from having trained nurses or other auxiliary health care workers to provide routine care for minor illnesses. But we weren't there yet.

The only interesting case that hectic morning was a 20-year-old woman brought in by her brother. "She's been acting strangely," he told me.

"Can you be more specific?"

"She stays up too late, washes rocks, and talks nonsense."

Observing the woman's extreme restlessness and pressured speech, as well as her hypersexuality when she talked, we decided to admit her for manic psychosis – not that we had an appropriate ward for someone in her condition. She immediately began twisting, turning, sitting on the floor, standing up, trying anything to break free, and talking unintelligible Tibetan gibberish. It didn't take her long to slip away from her attendants. That afternoon, I found her brother trying to force her back into the hospital by kicking her from behind, pushing her, and pulling her hair. I had to restrain myself from getting too involved, but tried to separate her from him as I walked her back to the hospital. For all I knew, he or his family had contributed to her illness in the first place.

When we got her back in her room, she threw a glass straight through the window. I finally resorted to "Vitamin H," our code word for the powerful sedative haloperidol. I then turned to the brother and lectured him on the inappropriateness of abusing a mentally ill patient.

It was several days before I was able to take the woman to see an Indian psychiatrist, who recommended giving her five different medications – yes, five. In my residency we had a name for that kind of prescribing behavior, practiced by those who really don't know what to prescribe, so they prescribe one drug from each major class of medication - "polypharmacy." I became quite disconcerted when I saw his clinic sheet. Apparently he had only spent 10 minutes with her. I decided to stick with the haloperidol plus a drug to counteract the unwanted neurologic side effects of the strong sedative.

Just as I was heading for bed that night, a nurse called me down to see another mentally ill patient – a young woman from Sogar School. She had been complaining about severe abdominal pain for several hours and was now wriggling around, acting overly anxious, and repeatedly crying out, "Oh mother!" I checked her belly and found nothing of note. Then I remembered a recent conversation with a friend who did interviews for Amnesty International. She told me about a woman at Sogar School with the same name as the patient, "D." This woman had crossed the Himalayas pregnant and gone into premature labor on one of the high passes between Tibet and Nepal. The rest of her group did not want to stop and left her to labor alone in subzero temperatures with no shelter. The baby died shortly after being born, and "D" was nearly dead when a trekking guide found her.

"D" ended up in Namche Bazar, the traditional main staging area for teams attempting to ascend Mount Everest from Nepal. She was taken in by a Nepali family and granted refugee status by the United Nations High Commissioner for Refugees. Within a few days, a helicopter had brought her down to Katmandu, and she had eventually ended up at Sogar School. Could she be the same "D" who was now in my emergency room with inexplicable abdominal pain? I could only guess at how the psychological scars of such a traumatic experience might manifest physically.

"Are you 'D' from Namche Bazar?" I asked finally. She denied it, but after we calmed her down and tucked her in, her friends came over and whispered to me that she was the same "D" after all. I found it very humbling to be in the presence of someone with the fortitude to make it through such an extraordinarily difficult journey. My heart sagged. I could certainly not imagine how it must have felt. My only hope was that I could offer her the first-rate medical care that she deserved.

The following morning, we had quite a scare when a doctor from the Tibetan Medical Institute brought in a patient with a breech delivery in progress. One leg and part of the umbilical cord had prolapsed (slipped out) through her cervix. This was life-threatening – too much pressure on the cord could threaten the life of the child by depriving the baby of oxygen. A delivery is a stressful event for a baby, and to have this added stressor could result in brain damage. Bryan put the patient in a taxi and drove an hour with her through the windy Himalayan roads to the district hospital in Kangra, where there were obstetricians. The mother spent the entire drive with her backside in the air to keep the baby's weight off the cord. It turned out to be a therapeutic taxi ride. When they arrived, the cord had gone back inside the uterus. The mother delivered the baby vaginally without complication, and both were fine. You won't read about that intervention in the standard obstetrical textbooks!

When Bryan returned from his unexpected road trip, I was able to go on one of my own short field trips to check on TB patients in seven outlying Tibetan settlements in the state of Himachal Pradesh. On the first day, the trip took me hundreds of kilometers through cold rain along winding, potholed roads. Despite the dreary weather, I enjoyed driving through the Kulu Valley, which looked very much like a Swiss alpine valley except for the apple and plum orchards.

My most important stop was the large resort town of Manali, which was surrounded by 15,000-foot mountains, and home to a large Tibetan settlement. The town would have been incredibly picturesque if it weren't for dozens of large, garish Indian hotels and several shopping malls. Some of Manali's families were wealthy enough to have cable television, while others were dirt poor, but all were tremendously hospitable. Other than the weather, some bad food, and my first personal experience with the diarrhea-inducing parasite known as giardia, I enjoyed the opportunity to see more of the Indian countryside.

When I returned to Dharamsala, I found I had earned an entire week off for rest and relaxation. I decided to attend the spring *Monlam* teachings by the Dalai Lama. On my first day, I walked up the hill from our compound to the large courtyard in front of the main Namgyal temple and could hardly believe my eyes. There must have been 5,000 people waiting for the day's teachings to begin, all sitting in complete silence. It was a bit eerie at first, but comforting as well. About 1,000 of the guests appeared to be foreigners. Most had arrived early in the morning, as the competition for space was fierce. As I soon learned while looking for a place to sit, the American Buddhists (many of whom seemed to have New York accents) were the worst. Some put pillows or blankets on the ground to reserve their spot. If you happened to move their placeholder by accident, you were hit with a tirade of expletives and sometimes threatened with physical harm. It was not very Buddhist behavior, I must say. The Tibetans, on the other hand, shared everything in the spirit of interdependent existence. They demonstrated just the kindness, compassion, generosity, and equanimity that one would expect. They would practically give you their seat, their food, their blanket, and their kitchen sink (if they had one).

I inched my way along the wall and managed to secure a spot near Lakhdor, the Tibetan monk doing the English translation. The opening day's topics were perseverance and patience. I enjoyed the spiritual aspect of the teachings, a welcome respite from the hustle and bustle of my regular "day job." Though I did not think I could sit through extended teaching sessions, I looked forward to the week of being able to reflect on my experiences so far, and what I wanted to do with the remaining time I had. Amidst the repetitive Buddhist chants and structured rituals, I finally decided to help the torture survivors find better care, as best I could.

That afternoon, the Dalai Lama made an announcement: one of the Tibetans on the Peace March from Dharamsala to Delhi had been accidentally killed in the middle of the night. The march was originally scheduled to go from Delhi to Lhasa, but the Dalai Lama had urged a change of plans, saying he didn't want to see anyone get hurt by the Chinese when they tried to cross the border. Realistically, the marchers wouldn't have gotten through Nepal in the first place, let alone across the border into Tibet. So the organizers decided to march 18 hours a day along the main roads between Dharamsala and Delhi. Marching before the first light of day turned out to be a bad idea, however, considering the poor road safety in India. It was a traffic accident that killed the marcher. It reaffirmed my fears about the safety of the Indian highways. I hated to hear about traffic accidents, knowing full well that the next time it could be someone I knew, or me.

The Dalai Lama was visibly moved as he made the announcement. A few minutes later, he took another break from the teaching and quietly wept. The crowd was profoundly silent. I'm sure most had never seen their leader cry, let alone a world leader of peace and nonviolence.

I continued to attend the teachings for the next 2 days, but I have to admit both my backside and upside (the mind trying to reach enlightenment) began to grow numb at the end of each day. I left before lunch on the last day and on my way down the hill, I ran into an Englishwoman who seemed lost.

"Where are you trying to go?" I asked.

"I need to change some money."

"There's a bank in the lower town past the hospital. Follow me."

As we were walking down, she spied some friends of hers ahead and called out, "Koo! Richard!" Koo turned out to be the American film actress Koo Stark, a former movie star (credits include the Rocky Horror Picture Show and deleted scenes from Star Wars, plus other B-rate movies), who gave up her profession to become a philanthropist and Buddhist. Richard was none other than Richard Gere, the Hollywood actor who has devoted significant personal resources to helping the Tibetan cause. He had come for the teachings and was staying at the Kashmir Cottage just up the road from Delek Hospital. The Englishwoman who wanted to change money turned out to be Annabel Heseltine, a reporter for the London Times and daughter of Michael Heseltine, the man John Major slimly beat to become the British Prime Minister.

"I'm just going to the bank to change some money," Annabel said after we finished with the introductions.

"You could also change it with a friend I know, it's easier sometimes," Koo advised her. "You can get a slightly higher exchange rate that way." The advice seemed ironic from someone likely well off, but I decided to hold my tongue.

Annabel decided to stick with the bank, and I pointed her in the right direction. I wanted to ask a question of Richard Gere, whose answer in retrospect turned out to be very sage advice.

"Richard, I've been pondering visiting either Tibet or Ladakh when I'm through with my volunteer year at the hospital. Do you have any thoughts about this?"

"Go to Tibet," he said unequivocally. "The Chinese are destroying Tibet at an unrelenting pace. You should go before it changes irreparably. The population transfer, environmental destruction, and urban blight are depressing, but you should go to see it. Be a witness."

I decided right then and there to follow his directive and go to Tibet. Meanwhile, Koo had stepped into the hospital to use our bathroom. Her entrance caused quite a stir among the British physicians, among whom she was very well known. At one time she had been romantically linked to Prince Andrew, Duke of York, and her face had graced the front page of many English tabloids. Quite frankly, we were honored she chose to make use of our humble facilities. From then on, we respectfully called the bathroom "Koo's Loo."[17]

When the week-long teachings were over, I met with the local welfare officer to ask whether he had received directives from the Information Office concerning the employment of Bihari children in McLeod Ganj. He had received a forwarded copy of my letter and, in fact, had called a community-wide meeting because of it. I was thrilled that my efforts appeared to be making a difference.

"We are encouraging all Tibetans to reduce the use of Indian boys and girls for labor," he told me. That sounded good. What he said next was less reassuring. "For those who do employ children, we are instructing them to take good care of the children, clothe them, treat them well, and try to give them an education."

A well-treated, well-clothed child laborer is still a child laborer, I wanted to point out. Didn't the welfare officer understand that child labor – no matter how the child was treated – was a violation of Indian law? Encouraging Tibetans to take good care of their underage employees might signal tacit acceptance of their use. I left the meeting a bit disappointed, but also energized. Progress had been made, but there was obviously more work to be done.

With only 2 days left to my week off from hospital duties, I decided to devote some time to my human rights project with torture survivors. With the help of my translator Kelsang, I planned to interview nuns and students who had been tortured by the Chinese before escaping from Tibet. Though monks had also suffered the same fate, the media had paid attention to their stories already. I wanted to reach those whose stories had not been heard.

During my clinic time, I had met several nuns who had endured torture in Tibet. Some showed signs of depression and anxiety, but many did not. When asked, most credited their Buddhist beliefs for their resilience. To explore this further, I discussed the phenomenon with Tenzin Choegyal, the Dalai Lama's brother. Together we identi-

---

[17] "Loo" is British slang for "toilet."

fied several factors that may result in heightened resistance to mental health stress, namely compassion for your enemy (their ignorance and hatred), motivation for a cause (political or religious), and the acceptance of cause and effect (karma).

While the resilience of some Tibetans in the face of pain and suffering was remarkable, I knew that many torture survivors did have lasting emotional and psychological scars. If enough of those survivors could be identified, perhaps more resources would be devoted to mental health programs. Toward that end, I worked with Dr. Tsetan to translate the *Hopkins Checklist-25* mental health questionnaire into Tibetan. Translating mental health questions into a non-Western language was not as easy as it might sound. The hegemonic Western concepts of mind and psychiatry are often completely alien to Eastern cultures. Hearing voices, for instance, might be considered normal in some cultures, whereas in the West such behavior would be labeled either schizophrenic or clairvoyant. We had to adapt the language to the cultural context and validate the questionnaire by administering it to several key advisors in the community. It turned out to be one of the toughest aspects of my project. After three rounds of writes and rewrites, we finally had a working document.

Once we finished translating and printing the questionnaires, I took a day and a half off to attend a Yak Band concert weekend. Up the hill in the main town, more than 600 people squeezed into the performing arts auditorium, where a huge banner over the stage read, "INDEPENDENCE ONLY!" The band's best tune, a rock-and-roll song called "*Rangzen,*" or "Freedom," kicked off the night. It was thrilling to watch so many monks dancing and shouting in their off hours. The concert had all the energy of a Western rock concert, minus the mosh pit.

The following week brought the first of April, and the volunteers of Delek Hospital couldn't resist the chance to play an old-time April Fool's joke on Bryan. Nathalie got the nurse to call him down for a supposed emergency, and we all gathered on the second-floor patio. We each held a bucket of water. Little did we know that Bryan had gone to get his morning tea and bread. When he finally walked up the stairs, he was hit by a deluge of water similar in kind to the monsoons of August. Six full buckets of cold water ended up soaking the poor fellow and his breakfast. In a way, we were getting him back for almost burning down the hospital earlier in the year. Needless to say, his bread got a little soggy and his tea quite diluted. He knew he deserved it, and laughed almost as hard as we did at his temporary misfortune.

Unfortunately, April did not bring sunshine, but stinging hail. The sky was so black during the first 2 weeks of spring that I couldn't even see the adjacent mountains. The surreal forks of lightning were spectacular, however, and I enjoyed watching the thunderclouds roll across the valley from my perch above the Kangra Valley.

There were a few signs that winter was preparing to take its leave. The rhododendrons began to bloom fire-engine red. The smell of oleander drifted past my window. Flocks of parakeets occasionally flew by, a blur of incandescent green. The magpies graced the air with foot-long blue-and-white tails that any musketeer would covet for his or her fedora. And then there was the petite fairy bluebird with the most beautiful turquoise feathers I had ever seen. I could hardly wait for the moment when I could once again admire the flora and fauna from the hospital's sunny porch, without the warm fleece jacket that had been my constant companion since December, even inside my room. In the mean time, I was content to watch the storms while munching on my grandmother's Christmas cookies that she had packed in marshmallows to avoid breakage. They had finally reached me 4 months late – a bit stale, but still a godsend.

As the weather slowly began to warm, the flies arrived in droves. We tried to cover all the garbage bins, but the exasperating insects managed to reproduce exponentially in our exam rooms, filling the air with a noisome buzz. I mistakenly squashed a fat one lying sleepily on the floor, unfortunately in front of one of the nurses, who then screamed out in horror. Like most Tibetans, she believed every living creature was reincarnated from a previous life. I might have just squashed Teddy Roosevelt or Richard Nixon or Jawaharlal Nehru (the founder of modern India) for that matter. The nurse's horror didn't shake me. Despite living in the center of Tibetan Buddhism, I still believed a fly was a fly was a fly, and a disease-carrying one at that. It was a point I had debated endlessly with my friend Karma Khedup, a monk who worked at the Tibetan Library. I never wavered in my public health conviction about the danger of insects.

Although I was once again working a full schedule at the hospital, I finally found time to put my newly translated mental health questionnaire to use. I began interviewing torture survivors to determine who might need urgent medical or psychiatric care. Most of the survivors I met with were Tibetan nuns who had been imprisoned by the Chinese for 6 months to one year for "crimes" such as participating in demonstrations, singing Tibetan independence songs, or possessing books about the Dalai Lama.

Listening to their stories was never easy. It was terrible to visualize any human being, particularly a gentle Tibetan nun, being subjected to electric shocks or forced to stand in the cold for extended periods of time. The hardest stories were those of sexual abuse; some nuns were raped with blunt instruments or forced to disrobe in front of Chinese soldiers. Sitting across from these survivors as they shared their experiences, I empathized with their suffering. I could not even begin to imagine what they had felt. I can only tell you what I felt – disgust toward those who had caused so much suffering and awe for those who had endured it.

One of the most dramatic stories was that of Jampa, a 23-year-old nun who lived near Delek Hospital at the Shungseb Nunnery. She had seen me several times in clinic with complaints of "body pain." I suspected she was a torture survivor and, with the help of a translator, I eventually learned her whole story.

Jampa was born to a family of nomads in a region of northeastern Tibet called Amdo. She never had the chance to go to school. As a young child, she spent her days looking after the family animals and helping in the fields. At age 12, her parents sent her to become a nun in a nearby nunnery. She lived there until she was 17, when she made a pilgrimage to Lhasa and did tens of thousands of prostrations in front of the holiest Buddhist temple in Tibet, the Tsuglagkhang, to increase her karma.

During her stay in Lhasa, Jampa joined several other nuns who had become politically active. She secretly put up posters calling for Tibetan independence and eventually organized a large demonstration. During the fracas, she threw a stone at a Chinese policeman and knocked him over. The police arrested her and one of her friends and took them to Shechou Prison.

On arrival, the two nuns were stripped naked, beaten all over their bodies, and shocked repeatedly with an electric cattle prod. Jampa was told that her crime was hitting the policeman with a stone, and if he died, she would be killed. The women were taken to a shared cell with no mattress and only a basin to use as a toilet.

The guards often kept Jampa in shackles and forced her to wear a cold, wet blanket to wear down her health. They took blood from her against her will, telling her it would be used "for the people." They urinated on her and kicked her and punched her repeatedly. They shocked her with a cattle prod nearly every day and beat her with thorn branches and belts. Sometimes they attached her fingers to small wire traps and suspended her from the ceiling for hours at a time. Once they lit a fire under her, and she vividly recalled the thick, red smoke curling toward her legs. Several times, she was forced to watch a film showing a Tibetan monk being nailed to wooden boards and burned to death. She didn't know how old the film was, and it looked very real to her.

After more than 6 months of this type of torture, Jampa and her friend were told that the policeman had lived. They were never formally charged with a crime or taken to trial. Yet, they were sentenced to 7 years in prison. A week later, a high Chinese official came to inspect the prison. He turned out to be Tibetan and expressed surprise at finding the two nuns among the prison's most hardened Chinese criminals. By this point, Jampa and her friend had bruises all over their bodies and were nearly broken down. The official took pity on them. He ordered them to go wash his car, and then quietly suggested they run away quickly while the Chinese guards were out to lunch. They never found out what happened to the official.

The two women escaped into the nearby fields, hid in some haystacks, and fled by night into the mountains south of Lhasa. They heard there was a reward out for their capture, and that the Tibetan official who had helped them claimed he thought that they were prison workers. Several Tibetan farmers helped the women as they fled, though one man admitted the reward was hard to pass up.

Their escape route took them south of Lhasa, over the Himalayas near Kanchenjunga (the third highest mountain in the world) into the Indian state of Sikkim, a recently annexed kingdom in northeastern India. There they ran into some nomads, who told them they would be treated well if they gave themselves up to the Indian police. The nomads took them to the police, who put them into custody for not having the correct refugee papers. Jampa and her friend spent 8 months in Indian custody, after which the Indian police took them back to the Tibetan border. Instead of going back into Tibet, where they were wanted criminals, the nuns returned to Sikkim. The Indian police caught them again and put them in detention for 4 more months. According to Jampa, the Indian police were nice and treated them well, but insisted on taking them back to the Tibetan border once again. When the pair fled to India a third time, they ended up spending a year and 3 months in a Sikkimese jail in Gangtok.

While the United Nations High Commissioner for Refugees offered special recognition for Tibetans fleeing from Tibet, the refugees had to be certified by the UNHCR officer in Kathmandu as true Tibetans fleeing persecution or hardship. Jampa and her friend had apparently taken the wrong escape route out of Tibet. The Indian police never brought the women to the attention of UNHCR and eventually took them back to the Tibetan border for the third time. On try number four, Jampa and her friend took a different route into India and finally made their way to Dharamsala, where they were recognized as true refugees. They had arrived the previous summer, about the same time I did.

In addition to interviewing nuns, I spoke with several students at Sogar School who had been imprisoned by the Chinese. Two had been soldiers in the Chinese army for several years in the late 1980s. When the young men were called upon to control rioting crowds during a Tibetan independence rally in 1989, they were moved by the nationalism displayed by their fellow Tibetans. In an impulsive moment of loyalty to Tibet, they freed truckloads of captured nuns. They were discovered, imprisoned, tortured severely for several months, and sent to a hard labor prison camp for 5 years. The two had walked across the Himalayas during the last year and were now studying Tibetan and English at Sogar School. Despite their limited political commitment and lack of religious training, they seemed to suffer very little psychological damage from the abuse they had endured.

One of the most inspiring survivors I interviewed was an incredibly compassionate monk named Palden Gyatso. He had lived through 33 years of brutal torture and neglect in Chinese prisons. At one point, he ate his coat to stay alive. Yet, he still claimed to have no hatred for the Chinese. He saw his own suffering as a means to further the goal of Tibetan independence.

"I'm glad this happened to me," he told me. "Otherwise I wouldn't have had a story to tell the United Nations."

For my human rights project, I managed to interview 28 refugee nuns and 7 students who had reported a history of being arrested and tortured while in Tibet. In order to make a scientific comparison, I also interviewed 35 nuns and students of similar age, who had not been arrested or tortured. This group served as the "control" group, to which I could compare the level of mental health symptoms and make conclusions about the role of torture in their mental well-being.

Not surprisingly, the two groups were remarkably similar, except for the fact that the torture survivors had been more politically active while living in Tibet. More than 50 percent of both groups reported being persecuted in Tibet, and enduring physical hardship during their refugee flight. Among the torture survivors, the average age was 26, but they had been out of Tibet an average of 4 years. They reported an average length of captivity of 21 months, and 57 percent reported an average of 5 weeks of solitary confinement. Most of the abuse they recalled happened within the first month of being arrested and held in prison. Only 43 percent were charged with a crime, and only 7 percent experienced a trial. It was a sobering testament to the sad state of affairs of the legal system set up by the Chinese in Tibet, with no protection for those who were detained for political reasons.

What I discovered about their experiences of torture was sobering. The 35 survivors recalled being subjected to an average of 13 different types of torture. Almost 90 percent of the torture survivors reported experiencing electric shocks to their body, as well as forced standing and physical abuse. Two-thirds reported being stripped naked and exposed to bright sunshine for long periods of time. Fifty percent reported being held in handcuffs, being stood upon, having blood extracted by a needle without their consent, and being subjected to sleep deprivation. A third reported being forced to watch others being tortured, and having threats leveled against their family if they didn't coöperate. Less commonly reported experiences were being put in shackles, being burned by a cigarette on the skin, and getting beaten on the soles of their feet. Two nuns even reported being raped by electric cattle prods. Fifty percent had required medical attention and been attended to by a physician while in prison! It was a gruesome list to compile.

What I learned about the state of their mental health was revealing, and provided additional evidence that I later published in the medical literature about the lasting damage that torture can do to one's long-term mental health. Among both groups, those tortured and those not, 40 percent had elevated symptoms suggestive of anxiety disorder, and 14 percent had symptoms suggestive of depression. I attributed much of these elevated levels of mental health disorders to their flight from their homeland and status as refugees in India. However, 54 percent of the torture survivor group had symptoms of anxiety, markedly more than the 29 percent of the nontortured group. Anxiety symptoms were more common among those who were detained the longest, in those lacking prior knowledge that they might be tortured when they were arrested, among those who felt hopeless while in prison, and in those who had most recently arrived in India. Depression was more common in men, in those who were abused the longest, in those who were in solitary confinement, and in those who were not politically involved before they got arrested. My results suggested that torture has long-term consequences on mental health over and above the effects of being uprooted, fleeing one's country, and living in exile.[18]

What I found just as fascinating was the fact that 60 percent of both groups did not have signs of anxiety or depression. The answer may have been the fact that everyone was provided with adequate social support, either by international nongovernmental groups or their exiled government. All had room, board, and education provided, and most were able to continue functioning in their social roles. Social and cultural support is known to alleviate depression and stress by restoring ties to community while facilitating coping with the myriad of stressors of refugee flight and resettlement. Reconstruction of social networks, cultural institutions, and respect for human rights is paramount.

I interviewed each person attentively, and asked about their religious and political belief systems. I was completely fascinated by their responses. Tibetans are a strong people. Those who remained behind in Tibet have withstood decades of abuse and mistreatment, leading some to brave the dangerous route out of Tibet to seek safe haven in India. Even among those who experienced torture in their homeland, their resilience seemed to come from basic political beliefs about freedom for Tibet, and from the fundamental principles of Buddhism itself. Their resilience seemed to have an external dimension, an ability to respond to changes in the world, and an internal dimension, a means of gauging one's capacity to respond to external situations. I began to understand that those who are the most resilient are those who engage in action based on a metaphysical, inner understanding of their place in life.

I learned these insights from the torture survivors themselves. Many of the nuns I interviewed who endured harsh imprisonment

---

[18] In a subsequent case control study of 76 imprisoned and 74 nonimprisoned Tibetan refugees by Crescenzi et al, 63 percent of interviewed torture survivors had elevated rates of anxiety, and 57 percent had elevated rate of depression. They found that poor mental health status was related to a reported experience of traumatic events, material/social losses from being a refugee, acculturative stress, and adjustment to refugee status in the host country.

and torture spoke about their political acts of demonstration against Chinese occupation as sacrifice for their country.

"When I demonstrated, I was prepared to sacrifice my life for the good of the country, I was ready to die for Tibet."

"My contribution to the struggle is my body, so whatever happens to it is inconsequential."

"They could torture my body but they could not torture my free spirit."

"I did not feel bad when I was beaten, only when I saw others beaten."

"I should make good use of my body in this life, therefore being killed would be a small thing for me to do for the benefit of the nation."

To them, suffering was deserved and beneficial, for it increased ones' karma for the next life. The subjective meaning of their experience had both profound spiritual and political significance for many of the subjects. I was convinced that it helped to alleviate subsequent mental health symptoms they could experience after their release, or after fleeing their beloved country.

I put together a small presentation of my preliminary findings for the staff of the Ministry of Health, and they listened attentively. Many foreign organizations and human rights groups had come to Dharamsala before to collect stories of torture to report to the outside world, but few had ever made the connection to the health of those who had been abused, let alone made a scientifically directed study of the issue. My main concern was that the findings would eventually help the nuns who were suffering from the abuse so that they would get the treatment they needed and deserved. The local Tibetan Nuns Project, a U.S.-based non-profit organization supporting the Tibetan nun community, had paid special attention to those whom they thought were depressed or anxious. But the government hadn't yet allocated much money to the newly established torture survivors program run by the Tibetan Government-in-Exile's Ministry of Health.

The most gratifying part of my project was that it did put new life into the torture survivors program. Up to that point, the program had only registered six patients, which was obviously not an accurate reflection of the number of persons who needed its services. Out of 150,000 Tibetans who had fled Tibet since 1959, the estimate was that 10 percent had been exposed to trauma or abuse. The long-term effect of this on the Tibetan community was really not known. In refugee situations or long-term humanitarian crises, mental health services typically receive a low priority. I think this is partly due to the pervasive view that mental health disorders are signs of weakness or reduced resilience, of being less than a whole person.

Of the nuns I interviewed and examined, those found to be suffering from severe mental health stress were promptly referred to the Ministry's program through the Tibetan Nuns Project. Treating anxiety and depression appropriately takes time, and patience on behalf of the person's provider. I unfortunately left Dharamsala soon after my assessments were finished, and thus I never heard if any of the affected nuns got significantly better. I can only hope the treatment provided by the torture survivors program helped them find some measure of peace.

An elderly male Tibetan patient at the Elders Home.

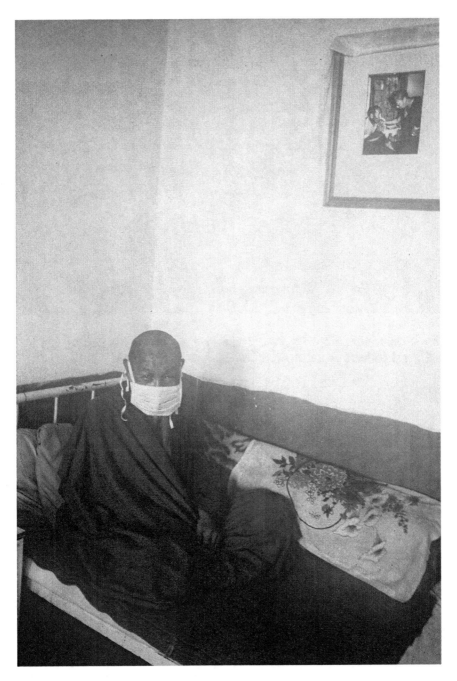

A Tibetan monk with TB rests in his room under a photo of the Dalai Lama.

The former monk Bagdro, still struggling with the long term side effects of torture in a Chinese prison.

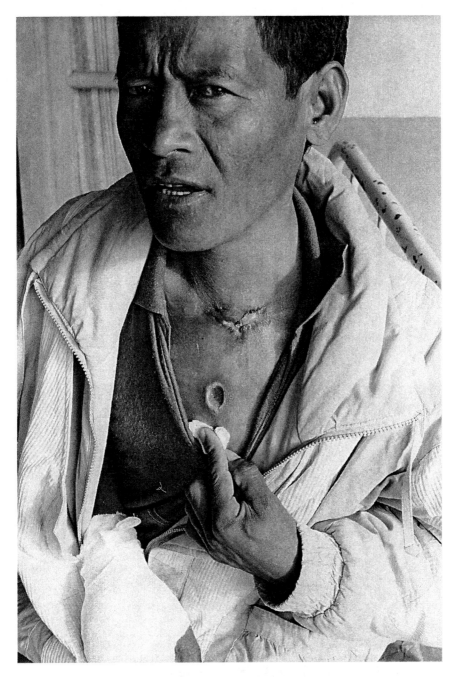

Tuberculosis can attack the body anywhere. This man had
tuberculosis in his lungs that had eaten through his chest wall.

A tuberculosis patient sits on her hospital bed, Delek Hospital.

Delek Hospital staff doing health education with Tibetan nuns in Dharamsala.

Palden Gyatso, who endured 33 years of mistreatment in a Chinese prison.

Dr. Tenzin Choedak of the Tibetan Medical and Astrological
Institute, imprisoned by the Chinese for 25 years.

12

Faith and Disbelief

As the spring temperatures in Dharamsala climbed, so did our patient load. Soon I was once again devoting nearly all of my time to clinical work. One reason for the flood of patients was the spring "monsoon" – otherwise known as tourist season. Dharma bums, mountain-climbers, curious-Georges, and loads of trekkers poured into town to bask in the Himalayan springtime and enjoy the closest thing to a Tibetan "Shangri-la" that they could find. Not surprisingly, given that we were in India, some of these folks got sick. Some tourists came straight to our door looking for immediate assistance, which we were glad to provide. Others were more stoic, or holistic, and took advantage of the handful of traditional Tibetan medical practitioners in town. After trying traditional Tibetan medicine for a while, many of these ill tourists showed up at Delek Hospital to salvage what was left of their health. This meant we often saw late presentations of common illnesses that could have been treated much more easily in an earlier stage. But our role was not to judge. Our duty as healers was to treat the infirm and the ill, no matter when they showed up at our door.

One of the more memorable tourists who nearly died from delaying treatment was a 25-year-old Englishman whose sole purpose in India appeared to be smoking marijuana in all the cool "hangout" places – the beaches of Goa, the mystical city of Puna, and, of course, the Himalayan mountains of Dharamsala. We figured this out after he collapsed on our front porch, and we searched through his belongings to find some identification. Instead we found a hand-drawn map with all his favorite marijuana dens in India marked with little cannabis symbols.

The young man's friends told us he had been treating a severe 3-week cough with Tibetan herbal medicine until he became incoherent and weak. Now he was in septic shock and practically comatose. To prevent his demise from a collapse in blood pressure, we quickly arranged a temporary intensive care unit with what we had available. An initial chest X-ray showed a complete "white-out" of his lung – his entire right chest was full of pus and fluid. Incredibly, the X-ray showed that there was so much pus on the right side that the pressure had pushed his heart almost all the way to his left chest wall.

Bryan, the doctor with the best surgical skills among us, acted fast. While the team watched, he inserted a chest drain tube into the man's right chest just under a rib, to access the fluid in the chest cavity. Bright green pus and liquid squirted out of the tube with such force that it hit the opposite wall with an audible "splat." The effect was about as close to bringing someone back from the brink of death as I'd ever seen. His blood pressure immediately returned to normal, and he became coherent again. He had no idea where he was at first, but we assured him that he was in good hands.

Within the first hour we had collected 3 liters of pus, a record at our hospital. A quick microbiology color stain of the fluid revealed streptococcal bacteria, an easily treated bacterial pneumonia which had gone terribly awry. We admitted the patient into our ward for intravenous fluids, gave him high doses of penicillin, and hoped for the best. Though streptococcal pneumonia is common and usually responds well to treatment, it can kill quickly if it's not treated promptly. This is what happened to Jim Henson, the creator of the Muppets, who died very rapidly from this same infection in 1990. With our patient, we were lucky. The antibiotics worked their magic, and he recovered slowly but surely. We didn't pull the drain out until 5 days later, after 7 liters had ultimately collected. By that time, the man's father had flown to India to find him and bring him back to England. It was a happy day for all when he walked out of our hospital.

Another memorable case of delayed care was an Englishwoman who had suffered painful ear infections for years, complete with draining pus and blood. She had tried Tibetan herbal medicine for this infectious disease problem and experienced mixed results. She finally came to the hospital when she couldn't handle the pain anymore. I took one look and realized she had damaged her eardrums beyond repair.

"It's time for some good old-fashioned antibiotics," I told her, and she acquiesced. I couldn't help but think how a course of antibiotics when the problem first began could have saved the woman years of pain, not to mention her eardrums.

I was certainly one to believe in complementary medical practice. I felt Tibetan medicine had much to offer patients suffering from chronic illnesses, beyond just chronic pain and mild psychiatric disorders. But when it came to infectious diseases, which were rife in India, I placed my faith in Western allopathic drugs such as life-saving antibiotics. I had seen too many ill people suffer due to a lack of effective medicine. I suppose I was a product of my own Western-oriented education, but I also considered myself pretty open-minded. Over my year in Dharamsala, I had developed a great respect for Tibetan medicine. However, many illnesses clearly responded better to Western drugs.

I kept all this in mind when a tall German man came in with a high fever and said, "I'd like you to respect the diagnosis of my Tibetan doctor." His voice was hoarse and wheezy.

"I will," I told him. I had made friends with some of the traditional practitioners in town. We respected each others' strengths and limitations. "What diagnosis did he give you?"

"He says my problem is a strong 'fire element.'"

"OK, we'll start with that." I answered. I was still in slightly familiar territory, but wasn't exactly sure how to treat a strong fire element. I probed for other possible causes of his symptoms. "Which vaccines did you get before coming to India?"

"None," he said. "I don't believe in them."

Arguably, there are vaccines that have low efficacy rates, such as those for cholera and TB, but I didn't feel that justified discrediting every vaccine. I didn't see the point in starting an argument, though, so I didn't bring it up. I suspected he might have typhoid, which can be very deadly to a person whose immune system has never seen the face of the typhoid bacteria before. After admitting him, I got him started on the oral antibiotic ciprofloxacin. "We need you to stay overnight, while we try to figure out exactly what's wrong," I told him.

He still had a high fever the next day, but he insisted on discharging himself against my advice. I heard later that he turned yellow and got very ill after leaving the hospital, but he refused to come back. Unfortunately, I never found out what the problem was or whether his Tibetan doctor was able to help him. I suspected that he didn't do well, which left me feeling both sad and frustrated. If he had had a little more confidence in the usefulness of antibiotics, he could have had a better chance at recovery.

I found it frustrating that so many of the tourists and settlers I met in Dharamsala believed that embracing Tibetan medicine required the complete rejection of Western (allopathic) medicine. That sort of dogmatism was possibly responsible for untimely and preventable deaths.

In mid-spring, I examined a French woman who came to Delek from Auroville, an alternative/spiritual/ecological-centered European community in the southern Indian state of Tamil Nadu. They billed themselves as a "universal town" where "men and women of all countries are able to live in peace and progressive harmony above all creeds, to realize human unity." I thought it sounded like a wonderful, altruistic idea, but I had doubts about their health model. The woman in front of me now had felt a lump in her breast 2 years earlier and decided to take Tibetan medicine from a famous Tibetan physician and author. It turned out that the lump was cancerous and the Tibetan medicine didn't work. When her breast began to ulcerate, she went back to France for a surgical opinion.

"They told me it was too late to operate," she said in a flat voice. "They recommended radiation, but I didn't want to do that. So I came back here and started taking my Tibetan medicines again."

By the time she came to see me, the lump had transformed into a huge, ulcerating cancer that had obliterated her left breast. It produced the worst odor emanating from a living person that I had ever smelled. I had never seen anything like it and never want to again. All I could do was help her with general hygiene, apply disinfectant, and give her antibiotics.

The woman's attitude was very unsettling. Of course it was her life, and she could make her own choices, but now she was on the verge of death at the age of 41 from a condition that could have been treated and probably sent into remission. I was certain she could have lived much longer with a lumpectomy or mastectomy. I wondered whether practitioners of Tibetan medicine should be offering treatments for cancer. No doubt Tibetan medicine could benefit cancer patients who were also receiving conventional treatments, but what could Tibetan herbal pills do on their own? I couldn't help but wonder why some patients put so much trust in herbal pills without even asking how they were supposed to work, or learning about whether they had been properly tested.

I had noticed a double standard when it came to questioning the effects of Tibetan and Western medicines. The foreigners I saw at Delek Hospital were usually quick to inquire about the effectiveness and potential drawbacks of any antibiotics or other medications I prescribed. In fact, I liked it when my patients asked me why I prescribed particular drugs, how they worked, and what side effects they might have. Yet, it seemed few people bothered to ask the same questions about the Tibetan medicines they used. Many patients took Tibetan pills without even asking what was inside them, blindly trusting that they were "natural" and therefore safe. The reality was that Tibetan medicine was not without its drawbacks. I had heard that some of the "herbal" pills might contain heavy metals, such as mercury, picked up in the manufacturing process of the medicine. In fact, a Tibetan pharmacist had recently died of acute renal failure, possibly because of an accumulation of these heavy metals.

The bottom line was that Tibetan medicine, like Western medicine, had its pros and cons. A stubborn, unquestioning acceptance or rejection of either system of healing was foolish. In my opinion, both systems had their place, and an integrative approach was likely to produce the best results.

Occasionally, I encountered a patient who agreed with this philosophy. One was a 50-year-old Buddhist nun from Spain, who had been taking Tibetan medicine for many years for chest pain, palpitations, and chronic anxiety. Her Tibetan doctor recently told her she had angina, a symptom of heart disease, and she wanted a second opinion. I think she recognized that heart disease was a realm where Western medicine might offer substantial benefits. It probably helped that her father was a cardiologist in Madrid.

As it turned out, the woman's cardiac exam was normal, and her symptoms were consistent with heightened anxiety rather than angina. I told her I doubted there was anything physically wrong with her, and she seemed relieved, but I was unsure how to proceed. What could I recommend to treat anxiety in a woman who was already taking Tibetan herbal medicine and meditating 5 hours per day? I was stuck.

Among doctors of Tibetan medicine, the nun's persistent anxiety would probably be diagnosed as *rlung*, a complicated condition related to depression introduced in Chapter 6. I had the opportunity to discuss the illness with the Dalai Lama's senior physician, Dr. Tenzin Choedak of the Tibetan Medical and Astrological Institute. Dr. Choedak, a robust man in his late 60s, had escaped from Tibet after serving nearly 25 years in prison for being a "counterrevolutionary." His left eye looked off to the left due to the torture he had endured in prison, but he had an infectious smile and an affable style. I found it humbling to sit in the presence of one of the foremost diagnosticians in the world, who, by feeling a patient's pulse or looking at his urine, could discern the inner workings of the human body.

Dr. Choedak was not a hard person to talk to, but it was hard to keep him on one subject. In his soft, raspy voice, he recounted the years spent in several Chinese gulags, the long periods of famine when he had to eat his leather hat and coat, and the reeducation classes by the Chinese.

"Many of my friends were executed," he told me. "Others died from unhappiness, even some of the high lamas."

I plied him on this point, for I was eager to learn more about the Tibetan belief in the connection between the heart and the mind.

"Unhappiness is the cause of many symptoms of mental illness," Dr. Choedak said, "from poor concentration to poor appetite to decreased interest in daily activities. Sleep is also disrupted."

"This is what is referred to as *rlung*?" I asked. It turned out that translating *rlung* as depression or anxiety was not quite accurate. For Tibetans, karma played a vital role in both physical and mental wellbeing. *rlung* could result from stressed karma, poor motivation, or wrong thinking.

"You must keep a right mind and right motivation" Dr. Choedak explained, "even when things aren't going well for you." That was apparently his key to surviving two and a half decades in Chinese captivity.

After my meeting with Dr. Choedak, I spoke with several of his colleagues about the role of Tibetan medicine in treating TB. They all agreed that Western medicine was best for treating new cases of TB, but some suggested that Tibetan medicine could help in drug-resistant cases. I was skeptical. How could herbs kill TB bacteria that had become resistant to the core anti-TB drugs like isoniazid, rifampin, ethambutol, streptomycin, and ciprofloxacin? I wanted to keep an open mind, but felt some collaborative studies were needed to suggest how best to integrate Tibetan and Western medicine in treating TB.

At least the Tibetan doctors agreed that TB patients should be sent to Delek Hospital more quickly, rather than spending days or weeks at the Tibetan Medical and Astrological Institute first. The problem was that some Tibetans, like many of the tourists, believed that Tibetan medicine was always superior. They felt Western medicine would sap their strength or throw their bodies out of balance. This belief led some Tibetans to refuse antibiotics and others to stop their TB treatments in midcourse.

One elderly man who quit his TB medicines later checked into the Tibetan Medical and Astrological Institute. He developed masses in his abdomen, and his hemoglobin plummeted to 3.5 milligrams per deciliter, an extremely low level. Despite his being at death's door, it was difficult to convince him to go to Delek for a blood transfusion. His family claimed it was the TB medicines that had made him sick. When he finally agreed to transfer to Delek, we had to give him 4 units of whole blood to boost his hemoglobin back to the normal range.

Sadly, children sometimes paid the price for this pervasive distrust of Western medicine. I felt heartbroken when a Tibetan couple brought in their 15-year-old daughter with a history of TB. The girl had experienced a seizure several nights earlier, followed by paralysis on her right side. She had also become delirious.

"Why didn't you bring her in right away?" I asked through our translator.

"We took her to a lama for a medical divination," the girl's father explained. "He said it would matter little whether we took her home or to the hospital. So we took her home."

When the couple finally brought their daughter to Delek Hospital, she was unconscious. Certain that she had TB in her brain, I put her on our antibiotics to cover her for both bacterial and TB meningitis. I had little hope of saving her. I was infuriated to see a young girl die because of the intransigence of her parents. If only it were possible to help the community understand that TB was often easy to treat with Western medicine, but not when patients came to the hospital as a last resort.

These kinds of cases happened with regularity. In a setting with poor access to health care, we often saw patients arriving late in the presentation of their disease. I had to keep reminding myself to be patient, that for many reasons the patients were not able to come earlier, or didn't have the resources that I was accustomed for my patients to have. In many respects, these problems were out of my control. What better place to teach myself patience than the center of Tibetan learning and scholarship!

I was told that the type of medical divination sought by the girl's family was common among Tibetans. Many patients consulted lamas to find out where to go for medical treatment and whether to take Western or Tibetan medicine. Divinations involved the interpretation of dreams, dough balls, dice, rosary beads, flames, butter lamps, or even bootstraps (a favorite of Tibetan nomads in the mountains). Some experienced diviners slaughtered sheep, removed and heated the shoulder blade, and read the lines on the bone. I admired the faith Tibetans put in their religious leaders when it came to medical care, but once again, I wondered whether they would be better served by combining the best of both paradigms. Why not consult a lama _and_ take antibiotics in the case of TB?

To some extent, Delek Hospital did go beyond a strictly Western approach to treating TB. In addition to conventional procedures and antibiotics, the staff relied on some therapies that could only be considered alternative. One of the oddest was a drug made from snake venom. It would be natural to think that this was an indigenously produced product, perhaps a staple of Tibetan medicine that had found its way into Delek Hospital's pharmacy. On the contrary, it was imported from Brazil where it was made from Amazon snakes. Called Botropase®, the drug was injected intramuscularly as a coagulant, especially in TB patients who were coughing blood. It was also supposed to be used before surgery to help stop bleeding.

The Tibetan doctors at Delek often asked patients' family members to buy a vial of Botropase® at one of the pharmacies in the bazaar. I must admit that I remained skeptical in the absence of a controlled scientific trial to see whether this stuff worked any better than a placebo. I was reluctant to give it the first time, for giving a drug that one had no experience with was nerve-wracking. Naturally, there was no package insert, just a blurb claiming the product was "totally atoxic and reaction free." I didn't think any drug could legitimately claim that. Rather than importing questionable therapies, I would have liked to see Delek Hospital engage in more collaboration with the local practitioners of Tibetan medicine.

I felt this was an important area for future research. I knew of no controlled studies comparing Tibetan and Western medicines in the treatment of specific conditions, or more importantly, how the two systems of medicine could be combined to maximize a patient's quality of life. In a community with a long history of and strong faith in Tibetan medicine, an integrative approach seemed most likely to give patients confidence in the medical care they received.

13

Never Easy to Depart

As my year in Dharamsala neared its end, I completed planning my visit to Tibet. I wanted to see firsthand the land that many of my colleagues and patients had left behind, a country most of them might never be able to call home again due to the ever-increasing Chinese occupation. I also wanted to see for myself how the Tibetans who had not fled were faring under Chinese rule. I have to admit the thought of seeing Lhasa with my own eyes was thrilling, and I could hardly wait to get there. Still, I tried to make the most of the remaining weeks of my volunteer term at Delek Hospital. This included learning some valuable medical lessons.

Unfortunately one of those lessons came at the expense of a local V.I.P. One of the highest personages in town was the Director of the Dialectic School, a lama in his late 60s who bore a striking resemblance to the corpulent icon of the Buddha himself. He was a high-spirited, active man and recently, a bit unlucky. One afternoon, while walking the *lingkor* path around the Dalai Lama's residence, he stumbled and fell 20 feet down the hillside and struck his head, nearly ripping off his right ear in the process. Bryan was on call that day, and sewed it back on rather deftly. He wrote in his chart to take out the stitches in 5 days (standard for the face/head). When the lama returned 6 days later, I was on call and removed the stitches.

A week later, the lama came back with his ear literally hanging on by a thread. What I hadn't realized was that cartilage is different from skin and needs about 10 days to heal, so I had taken out the stitches far too early – a tough lesson to learn by trial and error. I sewed the ear back on and made a note to wait twice as long before removing the stitches this time. The lama took all this in stride, and his ear healed without further complication. I was lucky to have such a jovial and understanding patient. In the U.S., this small mistake could have turned into a legal nightmare, with lawyers and suits and countersuits. One can not help but imagine that if everyone took the Buddhist attitude toward life, we would live in a much more harmonious and peaceful, or at least less litigious, world.

Another important lesson was less technical in nature – when it comes to the field of medicine, never assume you've seen it all. While this lesson was reinforced on a daily basis at Delek Hospital, a few incidents stood out. There was the Nepali road worker with a mass on his neck the size of a softball, most likely TB of the lymph nodes, or the psychotic monk who claimed the Chinese Army was lofting hand grenades onto his roof. Of course, no odd pathology – TB, psychosis, or otherwise – could compare to the story of the Scottish man who was electrocuted by a power line while riding on the roof of a local bus. His friends did CPR on top of the moving bus, then brought him to the hospital. His whole back had the look of a lightning bolt, and the bottoms of his feet were literally seared off. But he lived.

The funniest story of the year involved a young Indian road worker who staggered into the outpatient department one morning with labor pains, claiming to be 10 months pregnant. She had been working until the moment she went into labor. I was working my way through a busy clinic that morning, and had originally been told only that there was a new patient with "abdominal pain." Several patients later, when I took a look at her and realized she was pregnant, I rushed her upstairs to the inpatient ward and helped her into bed.

A few days before, Kevin had brought a new handheld Doppler (ultrasound) machine back from holiday in England, used for listening to fetal heart tones during labor. This was the first chance for the delivery team to try it out. We even called Dr. Tsetan down to show it off. It amplified the fetal heartbeat perfectly, much to everyone's happiness (including the laboring mother). During one particularly strong contraction, Dr. Tsetan placed the Doppler on the woman's belly to check for fetal distress. At the end of the contraction, the fetal heartbeat disappeared. Dr. Tsetan moved the Doppler along the mother's abdomen, but the heartbeat was nowhere to be found. Our team looked at each other with expectant worry, hoping that nothing tragic had happened during such an upbeat moment.

We stood bewildered for a moment, until Dr. Nyima lifted the blanket and realized the baby had delivered itself! The awkwardness of our mistake aside, we started laughing so hard we were practically rolling on the floor. It was hard to tell if our faces were red from intense embarrassment or laughter. The woman probably went home and told her friends that the Delek Hospital doctors put a machine to her belly, which made a funny noise and caused her to deliver – the magic Doppler delivery machine. We figured that once word got out, expectant mothers would start banging down our doors in hopes of avoiding the hardship of a prolonged labor.

Alas, the Doppler did not work its magic during our next delivery, a baby who was stuck in the occipital-posterior, or "face-up," position. This made passage through the birth canal much more difficult. Bryan rotated the baby in utero and eventually finished the delivery with uterine forceps. The mother hemorrhaged several liters after the delivery of the placenta, and could easily have died, but the bleeding finally stopped. While I was sewing up her vaginal tears, the woman's husband asked the nurse to tell me not to sew up too much. I had to assure him I was not sewing up anything that was meant to remain open.

For some reason, my last few weeks at Delek Hospital coincided with a dramatic increase in patient load coupled with another debilitating staff shortage. I was frustrated that the hospital had to rely on the volunteer system of physician labor to adequately staff the inpatient ward and clinics. We were continually running one doctor short, leaving us all overworked. I tried to explain to the administration why the hospital needed more doctors, but the standard response was that they were worried about having "too many." This worry perplexed all of us volunteers, while we worked at least 70 hours per week just to keep up. It was not good for our own mental health. It's been well documented that physicians who work more than 80 hours per week are more prone to making medical errors, and also have problems with depression and drug abuse. As far as I could tell, none of us were depressed or hooked on drugs covertly, but I was concerned that the high work hours were not conducive to a healthy work relationship with the hospital.

At one point, I found myself running the outpatient clinic alone for 6 straight days, seeing 60 to 70 patients per day. I couldn't imagine how any doctor could provide adequate care under those circumstances. I pondered the first eight patients I saw that week: a young nun with bowel obstruction; an elderly man with congestive heart failure; an elderly man with angina (chest pain from the heart); a young woman coughing blood (probable TB); a middle-aged man with kidney disease and no medicine to treat it with; a Tibetan astrology teacher with probable anxiety disorder; a young girl with a heart defect who was running a fever (possible heart valve infection); a Spanish man with a slow pulse of 36 beats per minute.

I had only 6 to 8 minutes for each one of these patients – I felt it was medical madness. To be the best doctor I could be I would have needed a minimum of a quarter of an hour for each of those cases, if not more. In medical school, we would have been given several hours to adequately work up and present each one of these cases to our attending physicians. It was a long way, both literally and figuratively, from my classroom back in the Midwest.

It also didn't help when seemingly healthy people wanted to hang around the hospital for the fun of it. After I put a cast on a demanding Tibetan monk who was kicked in the shin during a soccer game, he told me he wasn't going to return to his monastery just yet. "Dr. Tim-la, I was thinking I should stay here for some time," he proclaimed.

I was taken aback. "You want to be admitted to our understaffed little hospital in the Himalayas for a minor tibia fracture? You'll be much better off at home. For one thing, you could catch TB in our hospital." I basically had to order him to go home so I could turn my attention back to the throngs waiting in line.

Over the course of the following 5 days, my outpatient clinic roster read like a medical encyclopedia. A sampling follows: amoebic dysentery, breast lumps, chest pains, diarrhea, esophageal ulcers, fractures, gastritis, hypertension, infertility, jaundice, knee injuries, lacerations, mumps, nosebleeds, open sores, parasites, rheumatic fever, seizure disorders, TB (of course), urinary tract infections, vaginal infections, worms, *Yersinia pestis* (the plague bacteria), and "zebras" (we really couldn't tell what it was!).

Most of the week was a blur, though there were some rewarding moments amidst the commotion of hundreds of sick refugees crowding into our clinic. One morning, I saw the cutest elderly Tibetan woman, who had untreated hypertension. Her blood pressure was 210/100, enough to cause a stroke in most people.

"We really need to get you started on some medication," I explained, at which point she stuck her tongue out at me. This means something entirely different than in the West. Tibetans stick out their tongues as a greeting and sign of respect. I smiled back at her.

"Is it alright if I keep doing my prostrations every day?" she asked. We then had a good discussion about how best to get her blood pressure under control.

The highlight of the week was my reunion with Tenzin. It was time for him to stop his medications after a 9-month course of treatment. He was obviously thrilled to be done with the regimen, and I shared his enthusiasm. There was nothing more satisfying than seeing a patient who was once at death's door make a full recovery. He was now back to his full monastic duties, chanting and studying alongside his fellow monks.

The evening of my last day running the outpatient clinic, I was on call as well, resulting in my near collapse after a 15-hour day. As luck would have it, it was not a dull call night. The onslaught of emergencies ranged from acute appendicitis to a string of injuries resulting from another power outage that left half the community in darkness. People were tripping and falling all over town. I was trying to fix up a man who had fallen into a hole in the street, when a 12-year-old boy was rushed in from the Tibetan Children's Village. He had fallen 40 feet off the ledge of a school building onto the concrete floor below (no lights and no railings on the ledge). The right side of his face was smashed in, both arms were broken in half, and he was vomiting blood. We stabilized him with dexamethasone, phenytoin, and ceftriaxone, and prepared to send him on the long drive to the teaching hospital in Chandigarh 7 hours away. It was the nearest place with anything resembling a trauma center.

Due to a sudden fuel shortage, not one jeep in town had a full tank of gas, so we had to go from jeep to jeep siphoning off enough diesel fuel to make the trip. Then came the challenge of finding a driver – most were drunk after attending a big wedding earlier that evening. The entire process of finding a driver and sufficient gasoline took 2 hours, and with every passing hour I had doubts about the boy's chances of survival. By the time he and his family left for the overnight drive, he was starting to show some signs of neurologic recovery, but he had a long way to go to recuperate from such a bad fall.

We later heard that the boy survived the drive and several days in the hospital, but eventually died. The head trauma he sustained from the fall was just too severe to overcome. The whole incident prompted us Delek physicians to write a letter to the Tibetan Children's Village asking them to install guard railings on all the balconies and ledges at the school, but I'm not sure if that ever occurred. It was a classic example of the public health maxim, "an ounce of prevention is worth a pound of cure."

Only the next day did I learn the reason for the fuel shortage that had delayed our emergency transfer. The government had closed a refinery near the Taj Mahal, because of concerns that the emissions might tarnish the landmark's white marble surfaces.

The following week, I was mainly on ward duties, which I thought might be relaxing after my chaotic week running the outpatient clinic. My hopes were dashed on the first night, when I spent more than 2 hours suturing the hands of the Tibetan Medical and Astrological Institute's noodle maker, who had caught his hands in the shredder. I had barely finished putting in the final stitch, when a 50-year-old monk with a drinking problem arrived from a settlement 3 hours away. He had fallen down while drinking and suffered a complex fracture of his lower left leg. We tried to keep him down in order to tend to his wounds, but he kept climbing off the bed to go to the toilet. We finally put a huge cast on his leg and put him in traction, not due to necessity but as a restraint. It seemed to work, as he calmed down once he saw our Rube Goldberg device holding his leg in a fixed position. Sometimes ingenuity and improvisation are the better halves of healing the sick.

The next night two monks were rushed in with ghastly injuries. They had been goofing around on the roof of their monastery and ended up falling 40 feet to the ground. One landed upon the other. The unfortunate one who ended up on the bottom died shortly after arriving at the hospital. The monk on top sustained only minor injuries. He was fine, but I couldn't help but wonder what kind of condition his karma would be in after landing on top of his friend. I'll never forget the sight of the monk who died. His face had been smashed in, and blood was gushing out of his mouth. Our primary care hospital just wasn't equipped to deal with such high-level trauma.

Nor were we prepared to morph into a neonatal intensive care unit when a 40-year-old Tibetan woman gave birth to premature twins, her eleventh and twelfth children. Both babies suffered from oxygen deficiency at birth and did not feed well their first day. The next day the older began having diarrhea and became dehydrated despite our attempts to feed him oral rehydration salts. By noon he was nearly unresponsive to stimulation, so I had to put in an extra small intravenous line and draw blood from a thread of a vein. Maybe Delek Hospital was not the right place for these neonates? He soon developed necrotizing enterocolitis, a serious gastrointestinal disease characterized by a huge belly. I sat by his bed for 2 hours one after-noon watching him take what I thought were his last breaths. It was one of my most anxious moments as a doctor. By sunset, he was tak-ing breast milk well but wasn't out of the dark.

Meanwhile, the other twin also started having diarrhea. At least the fontanel on his skull was not so sunken, signifying minimal fluid loss. We were able to get fluids into him the natural way, and he avoided intravenous feeding. In the end, they both survived, much to our joy. It was another reminder of the incredible resilience of the human body, and even more so, the human spirit. Whether or not our interventions helped, I can't be sure, but I like to think our efforts made a difference to that family.

Psychiatric care was another weak spot at Delek, as I have mentioned before. It was not all that unique to our health care setting, however, as mental health concerns are frequently neglected even in developed countries with adequate resources. We were challenged in our mental health capacity when a woman arrived in a minivan taxi with her friends, kicking and screaming, refusing to come in. They eventually gave up trying to coax her out of the taxi and left. I later found out that she had been having bizarre fits of hysteria, where she would lose contact with the conscious world, writhe around in pain, and not engage with anyone or even answer questions coherently. Her friends took her to a lama, who told them to throw out something valuable for she was overtaken by spirits. When that didn't work, the next advice offered from an unknown person was to let her be 'given' sexual intercourse as the cure. Fortunately cooler heads prevailed, and her friends took her back to the lama, who said to throw out another valuable item. Apparently she got better after some time, but likely never received an adequate mental health follow-up. From our perspective, the best care we could provide was to put her on antipsychotic medications and enlist the help of the Indian psychiatrist in town.

We were again caught off guard when a young man on therapy for drug-resistant TB had a psychotic reaction to his cycloserine, an expensive "second-line" drug for TB that has more side effects than more commonly used anti-TB medications. One night he tried to jump off the hospital's second floor balcony before several fellow patients stopped him. Despite our efforts to keep an eye on him, he managed to walk out of the hospital the next day. He went to a friend's apartment, found a rope, and attempted to hang himself from the door. His friends soon found him and cut him down. He was still breathing, so they brought him back to the hospital. It was a horrific sight – the man was rigid with dilated pupils, signs of permanent brain damage from oxygen deprivation. He was gasping for breath, and I thought he was all but dead. We had no way to intubate him, to put a tube into his lungs to aid his breathing. We spent the rest of the evening using every measure we had available to try to save him, but I was sure I would be woken up later with news of his death. He survived through the morning and eventually went on to finish his course of TB medication. Cases like these were nothing short of miracles.

Another TB dilemma I hadn't given much thought to was the condition's impact on school exams. I had been treating a 10-year-old girl for the past 2 months, and her latest sputum test showed she was still smear positive, with active bacteria seen on the slide. It meant she was still infectious and not on the road to recovery. When I told her she would have to be admitted, the girl's mother started weeping. "Her final exams are tomorrow," she wailed. "If she misses them, she'll be held back one year."

My choices were to admit her immediately despite the implications for her education, or to let her take her tests and admit her a day later, allowing her to continue spreading TB among the other schoolchildren for one more day. Though my medical teaching told me to take her out of the community to prevent her from spreading TB bacteria to other students, my heart told me that the social impact of her disease was likely already too big for a girl her age to handle. I let her take her exams and admitted her for observed treatment the next day.

The next afternoon, I held my final clinic at Sogar School. I had been pushing Lobsang to compile a master vaccine list so we could determine the immunization coverage (or non-coverage) at the school. He worked about as fast as molasses running sideways on that task. My guess was that he was scared of what the list would reveal, considering no one had ever previously asked him to do this. In his defense, it was extremely difficult to keep an up-to-date immunization record in a wildly fluctuating, transient refugee population. At the moment, there were about 150 new students with no vaccination history.

When we were finally able to calculate vaccine coverage rates for the school, they were:

diphtheria-tetanus vaccine:

First dose	63% of the children vaccinated
Second dose	44% of the children vaccinated
Third dose	4% of the children vaccinated

typhoid vaccine:

First dose	55% of the children vaccinated
Second dose	33% of the children vaccinated

measles vaccine:

First dose	0% of the children vaccinated

Considering that even most developing countries achieve vaccination coverage rates of 60%-70%, these rates were poor. Now that the Health Department had some concrete statistics, maybe the need to improve them would be more obvious.

After going over the vaccination rates, I had a long talk with Lobsang about what else he could do to improve the students' health, such as purifying the water again during monsoon season. He hadn't considered doing that, although it turned out that he had already started giving weekly chloroquine prophylaxis to protect the students from malaria, which was impressive. The chance of getting malaria in the foothills of the Himalaya, however, was slight compared to the incidence of water-borne infections.

When I gave my final health talk at Sogar School that afternoon, I decided to tackle the students' fondness for cigarettes. Many of the young men chose to spend their miniscule weekly allowance on cheap Indian cigarettes called *bedis*. They had no filter, making them even deadlier "cancer sticks" than the Western varieties. I was sensitive to the fact that these young men had few avenues of recreation, but felt it was my responsibility to get across the message that cigarettes were hurting them.

Typical of the reserved Tibetan nature, at first most of the students were unwilling to risk speaking up, despite my attempts at humor. I began creating a poster in Tibetan listing the "benefits" of smoking, such as yellow nails, smelly hair, bad breath, chronic cough, etc. Slowly they caught on. Then one fellow stood up and shouted into the microphone, "Smoking makes me feel good!" He was a hard act to follow, but I tried to go over all the harmful effects in a serious manner as well.

While trying to come up with a Tibetan translation of "cigarettes reduce sperm counts," no word could be found for sperm. In the process, one man stood up and gave the audience his rendition about female semen and male semen. I could see all of the women burying their heads in their laps. I didn't fully know what he had said until after the session when it was a little too late to correct the record – an important lesson in the value of a competent translator. At that point I wished I had been able to learn more Tibetan myself.

As usual, the most thoughtful questions came after the session. One woman handed me a note in Tibetan asking, "Why do companies continue to make and sell cigarettes when they are so harmful to health?" Another asked, "If smoking is bad, and we can't stop doing it, does that mean we're stupid?"

I explained about the normal human response to a drug, the addictive quality of tobacco, and the profit motive. Then I laid down the line, saying that by smoking they were setting themselves up to get sick and therefore hurting the Tibetan independence movement. That idea seemed to stick.

These health education talks topped the list of things I would miss when I returned home. People everywhere, especially those with limited access to health care, love to talk about their health issues. I found it gratifying to help inform students who were obviously thirsting for knowledge. As for the efficacy of this approach, I had no objective way to measure whether my talks led to actual improvements in the health of the students. I do believe I contributed to their understanding of general health topics. Perhaps it was a small contribution, but I felt it was an important one.

Because there was such high turnover at Sogar School, my efforts to train the community health workers probably had a more lasting impact than my interactions with the students. Teaching the teachers is often an effective way to drive long-term improvements in any community. In the realm of public health, this means empowering local health workers to educate their patients. Toward that end, I gave a series of lectures on heart disease, bites and stings, diarrhea, and general health education. It was my first chance to teach basic medical skills to health workers who had never studied medicine.

I feel the most important session was the one dealing with diarrhea and dehydration. Learning how to make and use oral rehydration salts gave the health workers a powerful and inexpensive tool for saving the lives of countless children. We finished the session with a practical lab demonstrating how the health workers could teach mothers to make oral rehydration salts from everyday ingredients to prevent their own children from dying of dehydration.

I was already on a high after the lecture series, when I ran into Tsering Gyaltsen, Secretary of the Department of Information and International Relations, on the street outside the hospital. He wanted to thank me for my activism in calling attention to the child labor problem. He said the Assembly of People's Deputies, which consisted of Tibetan representatives from settlements around India, had discussed the issue during a recent session. "They concluded that child labor must stop, and it must stop now," he said, though he didn't fill me in on all the details. It was a gratifying moment during my last week in the community.

That night, I had what was becoming a recurring nightmare. I was driving down the New Jersey Turnpike listening to Bruce Springsteen and the E Street Band. I passed the Walt Whitman and Harriet Tubman rest stops, but I couldn't figure out how to get off. I was stuck on the turnpike, and the whole world looked as if it were made of emotionless steel and concrete. Refineries were on the horizon, as far as the eye could see. There was no green, no snow-capped mountains, and no fresh air. Was I having anxiety about returning to the developed world? Maybe a little, but I certainly wasn't going to miss the fuel shortages, power outages, broken phone lines, and other inconveniences designed to torment an information-addict like myself. Of course I was a little ashamed of my silent grousing. Surrounded by heartbreaking inequalities, rampant TB, and the pain of torture survivors, I knew that temperamental fax machines and unreliable phones were not the pressing problems of the day.

After one year, I had only scratched the surface of the needs and desires of Dharamsala's Tibetan settlers. I knew there was so much more I could have done, so many loose ends I felt reluctant to pass on to the next set of volunteers. My disappointment was somewhat tempered by a conversation I had with my translator Kelsang, a woman from the Tibetan Library whom I had befriended. She was in control of the sole computer from Dharamsala from which I sent my e-mail for the year (before the town was overrun by internet shops). Kelsang was young but wise in her ways.[19]

"Kelsang, I really don't know if I've made a difference here. There are so many patients to be seen, just as many now as when I first arrived. In many ways it's almost as if no time has passed. Things are the same now as before."

"One year is not much time in the grand scheme of things," she said with mild reassurance. The Tibetans have been waiting for more than thirty-five years to go back to Tibet. One more year to them is not long.

"But I feel as if I'm leaving work undone. The small dent I might have made will be gone in a few weeks. I feel like it's not a good time to leave, there is so much more I could do," I pleaded.

"It's never a good time to leave, Dr. Tim. You have made an impression in this community, and that will not be forgotten."

And yet I was ready to head home. I had student loans to pay, a career to launch, my family to see. For the moment, I tried to take satisfaction in my small but tangible accomplishments: sewing up a few wounds, delivering a few healthy babies, raising awareness about child labor, helping to bring clean water and sanitation to Sogar School, and documenting the trauma of torture survivors, in the hopes of helping them receive treatment and live happier, more productive lives.

I learned a great deal during my year in Dharamsala, both personally and professionally. First, I was thankful to be able to spend time learning about the Tibetan culture and belief system, as well as about the people and their relationships. Their resilience and tenacity had been described to me by many before I had come to live in a Tibetan community, but it was humbling for me to witness it first

---

[19] Kelsang has since been elected as a Member of the Tibetan Parliament-in-Exile, as a representative from the Tibetan region of Amdo.

hand. This strength of spirit was most evident in the torture survivors that I met. Although a few were having a hard time coping, the vast majority were going about their usual lives, getting by day to day the best they could in this new and unfamiliar place they called home.

I came to realize that it was not always due to a lack of knowledge, or ignorance, about health problems that led Tibetans to become sick. The amount of resources that they had at their disposal to change their refugee situation, known as their 'agency' in anthropology, was scarce and thus also to blame. Despite the popularity of Tibetan Buddhism worldwide, and the appeal of His Holiness the Dalai Lama, the Tibetans were still a refugee population, a people in diaspora, with all the concomitant problems that accompany those who are separated from their homeland. In the end, despite all our training, physicians lack control over and the ability to predict what illnesses people will suffer from. By and large, we must stay as far away as we can from the "blame the victim" mentality. The forces that determine health and well-being are largely above the level of the individual, namely the "structural" nature of how society is organized, and are quite beyond the daily control of individuals. By this I mean who is in charge of a population, who makes decisions, and who controls the distribution and movement of people and resources.

My biggest lessons were personal and of an internal nature. I had grown and changed significantly as a person; I now looked at the world and understood other people's suffering through different eyes. I recognized that there are multiple levels of suffering. I might be able to relieve the superficial afflictions of this life, but the deeper wounds and suffering that people carry with them will take far longer. The deeper levels of suffering that the Dalai Lama speaks about, those of change and pervasive conditions, take a lifetime to correct (and the Tibetans would say "lifetimes"). Pulling the drowning victims out of the river takes some skill, but the best way for public health to relieve suffering is to determine how they are getting in the river in the first place. Are they falling in, or being pushed? The upstream causes are much more difficult to identify as well as to fix.

It hadn't taken me long to realize that a great many people, even in this small community on the vast Indian subcontinent, were making do with very little. Their basic human right — the right to live a dignified life — was being violated. The poor weren't asking for much. They were not asking for the latest digital music player or fancy laptop or fast car. Most of the folks I met just wanted a little more dignity, to be able to rest easy at night knowing that their children had food to eat, warm beds to sleep in, and a roof over their heads. Many were not lucky enough to have even those simple things. I began to appreciate what I had in life, and value it even more. I also learned to be more forgiving, and to give people a little more leeway. Tibetan refugees in India are largely just trying to get by, and we all needed to give them a little more room to make a few mistakes here and there. No one — neither refugee nor physician — has 20/20 foresight in the decisions they make.

I also learned to be patient, and to pay careful attention to people's stories and suggestions, because the patient often knows best. Good physicians don't rush to judgment or rush to order tests, but take the time to listen to their patients and work with them as a team, taking into account context as well as symptoms. I believe this experience and this knowledge made me a better physician.

As for the field of international health, I learned that becoming fully engaged in the local community is a prerequisite for having a genuine impact through health policies. Providing the best care requires not just medical expertise, but a firm understanding of the people, cultures, attitudes, institutions, and relationships that make a community tick. Maybe it's a cliché, but practicing good medicine — whether in a modern city or an impoverished refugee camp — is far more complex than opening up a magic medicine bag and handing out its contents. Living in Dharamsala for a year, I knew I had seen only the tip of the iceberg. There was far more to learn about improving public health for the Tibetans in exile. If I hoped to understand the community more fully, I would have to return. The Tibetans I met and cared for were not just my patients; their struggle as refugees now had a special place in my heart.

The Potala Palace in Lhasa, Tibet, is a powerful symbol for Tibetan self-determination. The square in front has been ripped up and expanded to make way for large Chinese functions and parades.

Three Tibetan women in Lhasa spinning their personal prayer wheels.

Gyantse, in southern Tibet near the Nepal-Tibet border, is an
ancient trading center but now a central staging ground for
Tibetans fleeing their country.

Tibetan monk with his *gya ling* (Tibetan oboe) inside the main Tsuglagkhang Temple in Lhasa, Tibet.

Monks during a ceremony at the main temple in Shigatse, southern Tibet.

Elder Tibetan man, Shigatse, Tibet.

Man and child in Sakya town in southern Tibet.

Tibetan children often take care of their younger siblings.

Epilogue

Once again, I had a reunion to attend in India. This time, however, it was both emotional and physical. Several years after serving as a staff physician for the Tibetan Delek Hospital, I decided that I wanted to go back to visit the staff I had become so fond of, as well as see the newly constructed hospital building. As luck would have it, that chance came sooner rather than later. Dr. Tsetan was still the Chief Medical Officer of the hospital, and in late 2007 he invited me to come back to give some lectures on the management of multidrug-resistant tuberculosis (MDR TB) – now my chosen medical and public health specialty. I jumped at the chance to return to Dharamsala to see what changes had taken place, and to visit the small Indian and Tibetan town that had impacted me so deeply years before.

My experience treating TB at Delek Hospital had definitely influenced my career track, so it was only fitting to return to repay the favor. After my year at Delek Hospital I had returned to Boston and continued to work as a general internist in primary care medicine at a community health center there. I enjoyed the mix of nationalities and ethnicities I treated (Southeast Asian, Russian, Irish, Caribbean) as well as the socioeconomic variety; the population was a mix of the uninsured, the underinsured, and the overinsured. The strength and resilience that I had seen in the imprisoned and tortured Tibetan monks and nuns inspired me to move forward in my human rights activism. To continue my work with torture survivors, I joined the Physicians for Human Rights Asylum Network (http://physiciansforhumanrights.org/), whose members provide medical and psychological examinations of asylum seekers who claim to have been tortured in their home country, and provide expert testimony at their asylum hearings in the U.S. The medical evaluations are often key evidence to support the asylum seeker's claim of persecution in their home country. I also became a founding member of a new non-profit organization, Doctors for Global Health (http://www.dghonline.org/), which accompanies people living in post-conflict and marginalized areas (in both developing and developed countries) in their struggle to implement primary health care and public health services, and to help restore human rights and social justice in their communities. Lastly, my year in Dharamsala also convinced me to choose public health as a profession, and led to my current job investigating on the epidemiology of MDR TB in Eastern Europe, Africa, and Asia.

Getting to Dharamsala is no easy trip. In the years since my time in India in the 1990s, a new market for domestic air travel had emerged there. The middle class was growing, and they needed a way to get around. This meant good news – I would no longer have to travel by local Indian bus to get to Dharamsala! I booked a transatlantic flight to India on a well-known Western carrier with ease, only to face challenges in booking the short-hop flight to Dharamsala. The upstart air carrier wasn't even registered with the International Air Transport Association, and did not accept payment with a credit card from outside of India.

Upon my arrival in Delhi, I saw that the domestic airport had failed to make the transition to the 21st century. The building looked like something out of the 1950s, with pale green stucco walls, peeling paint, well-worn tile floors, lax security, and an undecipherable disorganization. By mistake I left some medical scissors in my carry-on bag that morning, but to my surprise I was able to talk my way through security by telling the guard that I was a doctor. As I envisioned scenes that could occur with a pair of scissors on a plane, we were driven out to the ATR-42 (Avions de Transport Régional, a mid-range passenger and cargo transport prop plane) in a transfer bus that was coughing soot and ash and had seen better days. My only hope was that the flight to Gaggal Airport, down the mountain ridge from Dharamsala proper, would be less eventful. Certainly it had to be better than the 12-hour overnight bus ride to Delhi I repeatedly had to endure the year I spent at Delek Hospital, before the age of modern transport.

The plane was loaded from the rear door straight from the heated tarmac. As I inched my way up the aircraft cabin I noticed from behind a "simple Buddhist monk" sitting in seat 11A. To my great surprise, it was the Dalai Lama himself, surrounded by several governmental and monastic advisors. I froze in the aisle next to him, and managed to crack a smile. I searched my rusty and limited Tibetan vocabulary for a greeting. What does one say to the spiritual leader of millions of Buddhists worldwide, a winner of the Nobel Peace Prize, and an internationally recognized global symbol for nonviolent social change? I decided on a simple *"Tashi delek,"* and he responded in kind. I continued to inch up to my seat, incredulous that I would be so lucky as to fly back up to Dharamsala with the Dalai Lama on my plane. Surely, we were safe.

McLeod Ganj, or upper Dharamsala, was different, but the same. Signs of growth were everywhere. It might have been that I was there during a tourist high season, but there seemed to be more people, more gawkers, more foreigners, and many more domestic Indian tourists. Busloads more tourists. The whole town seemed more westernized and commercial, although the shops were now owned by Indians from Kashmir and Punjab states and not Tibetans. The streets were still dirty with brackish-water open trenches, trash was everywhere (Richard Gere's push for a more environmentally friendly McLeod Ganj town had apparently failed), and the lack of a ban on plastic bags meant that they littered the crowded streets like popcorn. Cell phone towers now sprouted out of the urban landscape that blanketed the hillside. New massive hotels clung to the sides of the McLeod Ganj ridge without any apparent support at all. A new mini-mall was being constructed near the main bus terminal, a space now so small and cramped as to have barely any room for a mini-bus to turn around. I worried that the next Himalayan earthquake, even a minor one, would bring it all to a smashing halt. I banished the thought from my mind.

Delek Hospital was different too. In 2000 the hospital expanded with the addition of a new building with larger hospital wards, now able to hold 35 general medical patients and 17 TB patients. The Italian Association for Solidarity Among People (AISPO), San Raffaele

Hospital (Milan, Italy) had provided much of the funding for this upgrade. The U.S.-based Friends of Tibetan Delek Hospital had purchased a badly needed automatic X-ray film processor, ultrasound machine, and a generator. On July 6, 2001, the new hospital began housing patients. In 2008 Delek Hospital currently employs 37 full-time staff, in addition to the Administrator, Chief Medical Officer, and volunteer physicians and dentists. They have the capacity to do their own ultrasound and endoscopic procedures now, unheard of when I volunteered there. Even the electrocardiogram machine was working! Progress had been made.

What had not changed appreciably, however, was the TB ward. I went on TB medical rounds with Dr. Tsetan in the same patient rooms I had been in years before. The patients could have very well been the same, as the rooms had not changed. Many patients had been in the hospital for months on end in the hopes of a cure, and a small proportion of them had experienced a recurrence of their TB, years after their first illness. Thus, some of the patients might very well have been the same ones I had treated. The patient rooms, housing four persons each, had bare and whitewashed walls save for the occasional picture of the Dalai Lama taped near the patient's bed. Each TB patient had a small collection of belongings on their tin metal table, cassette tapes of Bollywood songs, herbal Tibetan medicine balls, toothbrush and toiletries, Buddhist amulets, and spittoons for sputum collection.

Dr. Tsetan showed me the worst, most drug-resistant cases currently admitted to the ward. When I was a volunteer, I knew little about the combinations of drugs that are essential for curing someone with drug-resistant TB. Now that I study TB, including the serious drug-resistant form, for a living, I found each patient's condition on this ward of immediate interest. Dr. Tsetan estimated that this hospital alone treated about 50 new MDR TB cases this past year (or about 10% of all the TB cases in Tibetans in India – an extremely high rate). Only about 25% of those were in persons from the northern state of Himachal Pradesh, where Dharamsala is located. (For perspective, there are roughly 100 cases of MDR TB per year in the U.S., a country of 300 million people.) The rest of the Tibetan patients came from Tibetan settlements located all over India. Delek Hospital buys local Indian drugs, and now uses a laboratory in Mumbai (Bombay) to make the diagnosis of drug resistance in the confirmed TB cases. Eight MDR TB patients were on the ward now. Each successive patient we reviewed was resistant to more drugs than the one in the previous bed. Dr. Tsetan estimated that he cures only about 50% of the cases. Also on the ward were two patients with extensively drug-resistant cases (or "XDR TB," a disease my colleagues and I had helped identify and name in 2005), which is resistant to the best four drugs doctors have in their pharmaceutical arsenal. These two patients, in the final room, looked thin, physically wasted, and emotionally despondent. Unfortunately the hope for a cure in XDR TB patients is less than 50%, even when diagnosed and treated in the best Western hospitals. I felt dejected after seeing them and meeting their families, knowing there was little anyone could do to save them.

I felt my sadness lift a little after talking to the Tibetan nurses at Delek Hospital, many of whom were the same ones who had worked there in the 1990s. The doctors at the hospital come and go because they are largely volunteers from the West. This is also true for the few allopathically trained Tibetan doctors who work there. The nurses, however, are the backbone of the hospital. What keeps them there is a desire to help their community, and their dedication to a refugee population in need. After going on medical rounds for several days with them, and watching them care for the sick, I was once again in awe.

My return to Delek Hospital reignited what had been inside me all along, something that Dr. Tsetan calls the "spirit of Delek Hospital." Chiefly, it is the feeling of satisfaction one gets from volunteering one's time to a worthy effort, however small that service might seem in the present. Volunteering in solidarity with a community will bear fruit in the health of the people; this is particularly true about volunteering in a health project. It is applicable not just for doctors and nurses, but for everyone who contributes to the collective effort. For the ill person, a healing intervention brings with it the immediate assurance of relief from pain and suffering. It also guarantees the security of presence, the feeling that for that one short moment, all will be well. That presence is represented not just by the healer, but by all in the collective project. And I realized that this spirit will continue, as I dwelled on the words of the Dalai Lama, "as long as space endures."

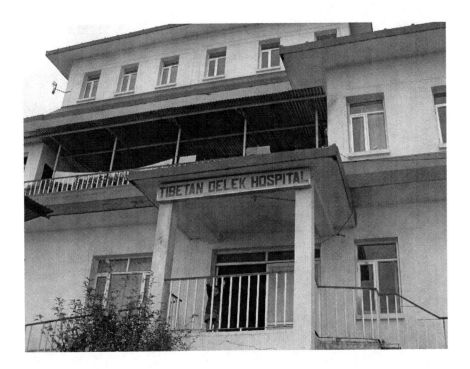

The new Tibetan Delek Hospital, with expanded hospital bed space and clinic services.

McLeod Ganj Community Health Center, upper Dharamsala.

The main bazaar road in McLeod Ganj, upper Dharamsala, home of the Tibetan community in exile, 2007.

The author, in front of the old Delek Hospital physicians' quarters, in 2007.

Ways to help

Tibetan Delek Hospital takes donations, as does the Department of Health of the Tibetan Government-in-Exile. Friends of Tibetan Delek Hospital is a U.S.-based nonprofit organization that works to improve health services at Delek Hospital. The Tibetan Nuns Project provides housing, medical care, food, education, and humanitarian aid to refugee Tibetan nuns from Tibet and other Himalayan regions of India.

Tibetan Delek Hospital
Gangchen Kyishong
Dharamsala – 176215
Himachal Pradesh, INDIA
+91-1892-222053
delek@sancharnet.in

Department of Health
Central Tibetan Administration
Gangchen Kyishong
Dharamsala – 176215
Himachal Pradesh, INDIA
+91-1892-222718
health@gov.tibet.net

Friends of Tibetan Delek Hospital
c/o The Tibet Fund
241 East 32nd St.
New York, NY 10016
+1-608-835-2222
http://www.delekhospital.org
http://tibetfund.org/delekhosp.html

Tibetan Nuns Project
619 Western Ave, PMB 22
Fourth Floor
Seattle, WA 98104
+1-206-652-8901
http://www.tnp.org

Selected Medical References on Tibetans

Bhatia S, Dranyi T, Rowley D. Tuberculosis among Tibetan refugees in India. *Social Science & Medicine* 2002;54:423-432.

Bhatia S, Dranyi T, Rowley D. A social and demographic study of Tibetan refugees in India. *Social Science & Medicine* 2002;54:411-422.

Bishop R, Litch JA. Medical tourism can do harm. British Medical Journal 2000;320:1017.

Dangerous Crossing 2003: Conditions Impacting the Flight Of Tibetan Refugees. Washington: International Campaign for Tibet, 2003: 1-20.

Crescenzi A, Ketzer E, Van Ommeren M, Phuntsok K, Komproe I, de Jong JT. Effect of political imprisonment and trauma history on recent Tibetan refugees in India. *Journal of Traumatic Stress* 2002;**15:**369-75.

Harris NS, Crawford PB, Yangzom Y, Pinzo L, Gyaltsen P, Hudes M. Nutritional and health status of Tibetan children living at high altitudes. *New England Journal of Medicine* 2001;**344:**341-7.

Holtz TH. Refugee trauma versus torture trauma: a retrospective controlled cohort study of Tibetan refugees. *Journal of Nervous and Mental Disease* 1998;**186:**24-34.

Holtz TH, Holmes, SM, Stonington S, Eisenberg L. Health is still social: contemporary examples in the age of the genome. *PLoS Medicine* 2006;3(10):e419-e422.

Janes CR. The health transition, global modernity and the crisis of traditional medicine: the Tibetan case. *Social Science & Medicine* 1999;48:1803-1820.

Janes CR. The transformation of Tibetan medicine. *Medical Anthropology Quarterly* 9(6):6-39.

Mercer SW, Ager A, Ruwanpura E. Psychosocial distress of Tibetans in exile: integrating western interventions with traditional beliefs and practice. *Social Science and Medicine* 2005;**60**:179-89.

Servan-Schreiber D, Le Lin B, Birmaher B. Prevalence of posttraumatic stress disorder and major depressive disorder in Tibetan refugee children. *Journal of the American Academy of Child and Adolescent Psychiatry* 1998;**37**:874-9.

Singh S. Tears from the land of snow: health and human rights in Tibet. *Lancet* 2004;**364**:1009.

Terheggen MA, Stroebe MS, Kleber RJ. Western conceptualizations and Eastern experience: a cross-cultural study of traumatic stress reactions among Tibetan refugees in India. *Journal of Traumatic Stress* 2001;**14**:391-403.

LaVergne, TN USA
25 August 2009
155823LV00004B/3/P